FAITH AT THE EDGE

Faith at the Edge

A Book for Doubters

ROBERT N. WENNBERG

William B. Eerdmans Publishing Company

Grand Rapids, Michigan

Wm. B. Eerdmans Publishing Co.
4035 Park East Court SE, Grand Rapids, Michigan, 49546
www.eerdmans.com

2018-11

Library of Congress Cataloging-in-Publication Data

Wennberg, Robert N.
Faith at the edge: a book for doubters / Robert N. Wennberg.
p.   cm.
ISBN 978-0-8028-6473-4 (pbk.: alk. paper)
1. Hidden God.   2. Faith.   I. Title.

BT180.H54W46   2009

231.7 — dc22

2009026539

For fellow members

of the Society of the Dislocated Thigh

Contents

Acknowledgments

xiii

INTRODUCTION

*Why There Is an Important Difference between Doubters,
Skeptics, and Seekers; Why This Is an Insider's Book;
Why the Chapters Are So Short*

xv

1

*Why Doubting and Questioning Differ;
Why Doubters Don't Always Question; Why Questioners
Don't Always Doubt*

1

2

*Why Truth Matters; Why Relativism Won't Help;
Why It's Important to Doubt in the Right Way*

9

3

Why Doubt Should Be Expected; Why Doubt Speaks Well of You; Why the Nonreligious also Doubt

20

4

Why Doubt Hits Hardest When It's First Experienced; Why It's Crucial to See Yourself as a Believer Who Is Tempted to Doubt, Not a Doubter Who Is Tempted to Believe

29

5

Why a Week with Mother Teresa Might Be Better for the Doubter Than a Week with C. S. Lewis

40

6

Why It's Important to Have a Theology of Divine Absence; Why It's Important to Have the Right Theology of Absence; Why C. S. Lewis Can Help Us

49

7

Why Saint John of the Cross Can Give Us a Big Assist; Why the Dark Night of the Soul Is a Blessing

59

8

Why Mother Teresa's Dark Night of the Soul
Has Much to Teach Us

69

9

Why Hope Can Be the Basis for Faith during Hard
Times; Why Hope Rather Than Doubt Should Guide
Our Lives; Why God Loves Hopers

81

10

Why the Christian Community Is the Best Place to
Doubt; Why Going to Church Matters Even
When You Get Little out of It

91

11

Why Unanswered Prayer Can Be a Problem; Why We
Should Love God More Than We Love What God Can Do
for Us; Why We Shouldn't Sell Prayer Short

99

12

Why It's Important to Come to Terms with the Fact That
Many People Reject What You Believe; Why
Disagreement Shouldn't Preclude Strong Commitment

109

13

*Why Not All Smart People Reject What You Believe; Why
Smart People Who Do Reject What You Believe
Isn't a Good Reason for Joining Them*

118

14

*Why Christians Aren't Always as Good as
Non-Christians; Why God Still Gets the Credit;
Why Christians Should Applaud Goodness
Wherever They Find It*

125

15

*Why God Doesn't Make His Presence More Obvious;
Why We Need to Come to Terms with This*

135

16

*Why Wintry Spiritual Types Can Be Profoundly
Spiritual; Why the Seasonal Nature of the Spiritual Life
Brings Us Both Winter and Summer*

144

17

*Why Concluding Remarks Do Not Come Easily; Why the
Dedication Page Finally Makes Sense; Why God Is Both
Our Adversary and Our Ally*

155

Acknowledgments

I owe a big debt of gratitude to a number of people whose assistance has been invaluable. Robert Gundry, New Testament scholar extraordinaire, and Shirley Mullen, historian and president of Houghton College, both good friends, have given my manuscript detailed attention. They have improved it immeasurably and have taught me much in the process. This is not the first time I have learned from them, and I hope it will not be the last. It could not reasonably be expected that they fix everything in need of fixing. So responsibility for what remains falls, as always, on the shoulders of the author. To my wife, Eleanore, who, though relatively doubt free, has patiently — oh, so patiently — typed and retyped the developing manuscript, many thanks. This reveals that things were done the old-fashioned way — ballpoint to legal pad to word processor. Then to my many students over the years who have stimulated my thoughts on this subject as they shared their struggles with me. I have in mind especially those who have struggled a bit longer and harder with their faith than some of their fellows. They are a marvelous group. I have enjoyed their company, teaching them and learning from them — in many cases well beyond their student years. Finally, one can only be grateful for the rich resources of the Christian tradition and for those men and women who over the centuries have lived lives of deep faith, lives not always untouched by faith's dark side, and who have reflected wisely and helpfully on the condition (not just a topic) discussed in this book. For the depository of works they have left us, we can only thank God. And, of course, there is Scripture, the Old and New Testaments, which is quoted from a variety of translations.

Why There Is an Important Difference between Doubters, Skeptics, and Seekers

Why This Is an Insider's Book

Why the Chapters Are So Short

This is a book for doubters. Not for skeptics. Not for seekers. Here's the difference. Doubters are believers struggling with their faith *within* the Christian tradition. Skeptics and seekers are both *outside* that tradition. Skeptics are critical and hostile. Seekers are questioning and open. Doubters occupy an altogether different place, uncertain about a faith to which they are no strangers and to which they have been committed, but who are now wondering whether it's true. It is their struggle of faith that concerns us in the pages that follow.

The topic, then, is what may be called "existential doubt." "Existential" emphasizes that this is not a merely academic questioning, an activity that can be pain-free — even enjoyable — at least for some of us. On the contrary, this doubt is very personal and deeply disturbing, famously called "the dark night of the soul" by the Christian mystic Saint John of the Cross. There are times — many or few, long or short — when God seems remote, when one doesn't feel God's presence in one's life, when God is experientially absent, when his very existence seems uncertain, when everything one believes as a Christian is called into serious question. These are trying times for persons of faith. What is at the very heart of their vision of human existence, life's point and purpose, has become disturbingly uncertain.

We face important questions. What causes our sense of divine absence and the deeply unsettling doubt that accompanies it? Is it our fault, or is there some other explanation for our uncertainty? Why does God allow this to happen in our lives? And how should we respond to this doubt and the sense of divine absence?

What we need is a credible theological account of what is happening to us. Something to help us understand why these dark episodes occur in our journey of faith. Something to help us cope with them, ultimately not be defeated by them, and even profit from them spiritually. For these dark times may not be just an unfortunate condition for which we need a remedy, like an unpleasant disease that needs curing so we can return to a normal state of health. They may be a normal part of faith's progression, something nearly all of us experience. Indeed, these dark episodes may not be so much a disease that needs to be cured as the cure for a disease. This is exactly what John of the Cross proposes. But for existential doubt to serve this good and beneficial purpose, it must be honestly looked at within the context of a mature Christian understanding. This we shall attempt to do with the generous help of others who have reflected long and hard and wisely on these matters.

A cluster of related spiritual challenges falls under the larger rubric "the dark night of the soul," and these challenges vary in character from person to person. Some people experience the dark night of the soul once and for all, in a single episode, never to be repeated but never to be forgotten. Others suffer through repeats, at least in the form of aftershocks, perhaps not so powerful as the original but challenging all the same. For some individuals the doubt and the darkness are never completely dispelled. One thinks of Mother Teresa, who had a lifelong struggle with the dark side of faith. Further, there is the challenge during these dark times, whether long or short, of maintaining a spiritual life that is true and faithful. How is one to remain a faithful follower of Jesus Christ during these periods? Is a significant spirituality even possible amidst such struggles? I strongly believe so.

This is not a book on apologetics, a systematic presentation of various arguments in support of Christian theism coupled with rebuttals directed at various objections. That would be a valuable undertaking. Indeed, for many years I have taught courses on apologetics. But apologetics does have its limitations. Christians experiencing existential doubt and a sense of divine absence more often than not need something other than, or at least in addition to, the standard fare offered by a text-book on apologetics. Doubters, unlike seekers and skeptics, are struggling within the context of a Christian faith they have accepted and have personally experienced. Their doubts are largely "insider" doubts: doubts generated, for example, by losing a strong sense of God's presence or by the failure of prayer to work in the way Scripture seems to say it works. The doubts of outsiders have a different character. Outsiders, whether skeptics or seekers, lack Christian experience. The challenges they direct at the Christian faith have to be met with arguments based on assumptions they can accept as nonbelievers.

Typically, apologetics is directed at the outsider's challenge. Seeking to meet that challenge is an honorable and profitable exercise, but when the dark night of the soul descends, a crash course in apologetics doesn't always help. Having severe doubts does not make one an outsider, with only the outsider's concerns, assumptions, and limited resources. As Simone Weil observes, "a religion is known only from the inside. . . . Religion is a form of nourishment. It is difficult to appreciate the flavor and food value of something one has never eaten."[1] Outsiders are experientially unacquainted with the power and attractions of the doubter's faith and therefore unacquainted with what prompts doubters to wrestle mightily with their doubts and sense of divine absence and not quickly abandon the

1. Simone Weil, *Waiting for God* (New York: Harper and Row, 1951), p. 183.

struggle in defeat. The outsider has not shared the deep Christian experience that the insider is now struggling to retain and renew. Also, insiders have available to them rich theological resources of the Christian tradition. So when C. S. Lewis or John of the Cross offer their interpretations of the divine absence, they are functioning as Christian thinkers, as insiders. They are offering us a theology of divine absence. They are attempting to make sense of the dark accompaniments of faith within the context of that faith. Skeptical outsiders will not accept what they have to say — nor necessarily should they — but the doubter, still an insider, will listen. This is an insider's book.

Just as this book is not an apologetics text, neither is it a piece of psychological counseling. Certainly there are times when that is just what is needed. Individuals may suffer from a clinical depression that seriously distorts how they see themselves and the world in which they live. When the darkness and despair associated with such depression descends, it will also envelop their spiritual vision, sapping its vitality, strength, and meaningfulness. When this happens, appropriate therapy is needed, not theological and philosophical ruminations on the nature of doubt. Therefore, what is assumed in what follows is a relatively healthy psyche, free from clinical depression as the cause of one's doubt and uncertainty. All of us, of course, can have our psychological down times, well short of what is labeled "clinical depression." This too can distort, though to a lesser degree, how we view our world and our faith. When we recognize one of those down times, wisdom would counsel us to defer important decisions or serious assessments of our commitments. Thankfully these typically don't last long. But depression does not cause the doubt for the existential doubter. The doubt causes the depression. It is this kind of doubt that we will reflect on in the pages ahead.

Sometimes introductions assist the reader in following an argument that is technical and rather complicated. The author provides a range of pointers to guide the reader through the book. But that is not necessary here, because there is no single line of reasoning that has to be followed step-by-step. Rather, what is offered is a series of reflections that we hope will help the reader, but that do not systematically build on one another so much as supplement one another. This gives the reader the freedom to embrace some but not all of what is said without the whole logical edifice collapsing. Nevertheless, there may be considerable advantage to reading the chapters in the order given. In some cases earlier observations, distinctions, and definitions help the reader gain a fuller understanding of what follows. So following the order provided is recommended.

The book consists of a series of chapters sufficiently short that they are perhaps better called something other than chapters, possibly "reflections." But that term can be misleading, suggesting informal, highly personal, and rather scattered thoughts on a variety of topics. Though I do not avoid personal illustrations in the book, what follows is not idiosyncratically personal in the sense of being disconnected from the wisdom and insights of others, such as John of the Cross, Blaise Pascal, G. K. Chesterton, Miguel de Unamuno, Simone Weil, C. S. Lewis, and Martin Marty. These are valuable resources and well worth drawing on, as I have done. My chapters are short for a simple reason: to provide manageable, "bite-size" sections that can be pondered, each making its own claim on our attention, and subject to the reader's own critical response and possible appropriation.

When writing a book, all authors are supposed to ask themselves a basic question: Who is your intended audience? Obviously my book is for doubters, and moreover, it is for those doubting souls who are right in the midst of their dark night, whose faith is currently at the edge. But it is also for past and future doubters as well. It may be an important resource for understanding and profiting spiritually from that dark night as one looks back on it, puzzles about it, and seeks to make some sense of it. For it is possible to reach back in time, reflect on those dark times of doubt in our Christian journey, and gain important insights that can be profitably applied to our present life of faith. The book is also for those who never seem quite able to shake completely free of their doubt and lack of a powerful, consoling sense of God's presence. Moreover, these reflections may also play an apologetical role as one seeks to figure out why God would allow such dark and unpleasant episodes to occur, especially when they are not typically a product of spiritual dereliction on the part of the person undergoing them. What theological sense can be made of them? Further, this book may be helpful to those who are doubt-free but want to understand their doubting brothers and sisters, though there is nothing like firsthand experience to bring real understanding. It may also contribute to a wider theological discussion of these matters, a discussion that has value apart from any immediate value the book might have as a primer for doubters. It is not, however, intended to foster doubt, as if every Christian should have a good dose of existential doubt and, by golly, I'm going to make sure he or she has it. Doubt doesn't need any help from me. It's doing quite well on its own. But it does need to be put in its place.

Existential doubters are neither a spiritually inferior nor a spiritually superior breed within the Christian community. They simply are. But they are to a considerable extent a neglected group, which probably means that many of us, if not most of us, are being neglected. And what is neglected is an important part of who we are and what we have experienced or are experiencing as Christians. In the pages that follow, I attempt to redress that neglect.

At the end of each chapter you will find questions. The one exception is the last chapter. These questions are meant not only to encourage and guide private reflection, but also to aid open discussion and interaction with others. Though the topic of this book is intensely personal, it is not a condition of heart and mind that is to be hidden away and dealt with in isolation — quite the opposite. However one goes about this, alone or with others or in some combination of the two, it is hoped that help and encouragement will be found in these pages.

1

Why Doubting and Questioning Differ

Why Doubters Don't Always Question

Why Questioners Don't Always Doubt

When we experience painful, distressing, and pro-longed uncertainty about the truth of what we be-lieve as Christians, we are experiencing "existential doubt." This is the real thing, not some fleeting low-grade doubt or some momentary questioning. It is painful and distressing because we are seriously experiencing uncer-tainty over the very beliefs around which we have sought to build our lives, the beliefs that have given direction and coherence to the lives we seek to live. These are be-liefs with which we have been publicly identified and that have given us our sense of identity. This is who we are, Christians, followers of Jesus Christ. And then suddenly we wonder — really wonder — is it all true?

Such doubt is more than doubt about abstract doc-trine. It is not merely a skeptical response to some theo-logical formulation or other. It is much more personal

1

than that. We are not suggesting, however, that doctrine is unimportant in the life of the Christian. Here we must be clear. Doctrine *is* crucially important. After all, doctrine shapes our understanding of God and provides us with an interpretation of our own spiritual experience. It is, we affirm, the God and Father of Jesus Christ whom we are encountering, not a deity with characteristics incompatible with the God we see in Jesus. Doctrine and biblical teaching guide us here. They both prompt and assist us in interpreting our religious experience. Nevertheless, there is more to existential doubt than doubt about biblical and theological doctrine, though that may be part of it. There is also a deep sense of personal loss. In this regard it is more like the pain we experience when a much-loved family member is seriously ill, suspended between life and death. We stand by in agonizing uncertainty over the fate of this one whom we love and who means so much to us. Will she or will she not survive? Existential doubt is more like that than uncertainty over abstract theological formulations. The concern is personal, not merely propositional. The poet John Crowe Ransom captures this sense of loss with these words.

> Two evils, monstrous either one apart
> Possessed me, and were long and loathe at going
> A cry of Absence, Absence in the heart
> And in the wood the furious winter blowing.[1]

1. Quoted in Martin E. Marty, *A Cry of Absence* (San Francisco: Harper and Row, 1983), p. 1. "Winter Remembered" from *Selected Poems* by John

"Absence" has been capitalized by Ransom, an indication that we are here concerned with God. The One who is absent is the One we want to be powerfully present so that we have no doubt and no uncertainty. But God's presence is just what we don't have. Rather, God is remote. Indeed, God is experientially nonexistent. We are undergoing the winter of the heart. This is "existential doubt." It could also quite appropriately be called "existential loss." Notice, further, that this Absence in the heart was, as Ransom puts it, "long and loathe at going." There was no quick fix. No "just get down on your knees and pray, read your Bible, confess your sin and all will be well." To be sure, these are all good things to do. Indeed, they are staples of the Christian life. But failing to sincerely engage in these activities typically is not (I won't say never) the *cause* of our distress, nor therefore is it typically (again, I won't say never) the *cure* for our distress. Matters are more complicated than that, as we shall see.

It is important from the outset to distinguish existential doubt from another kind of doubt. Let us call this other doubt "theoretical doubt." Though they are different, there may be certain crucial connections. The one, theoretical doubt, can give rise to the other, though it need not do so and often does not. Theoretical doubt is a

Crowe Ransom, copyright 1924 by Alfred A. Knopf, a division of Random House, Inc. and renewed 1952 by John Crowe Ransom. Used by permission of Alfred A. Knopf, a division of Random House, Inc. John Crowe Ransom, "Winter Remembered" from *Selected Poems* (Manchester: Carcanet Press Limited, 1991).

kind of intellectual puzzlement or questioning. Indeed, it is possible to be perplexed about something you believe to be true, raise questions about it, and all the while be completely confident of its truth. This is by no means a rare phenomenon. It happens all the time. Thus, "I don't care what you say or what anyone else says or for that matter what *everyone* else says, I know it's wrong to torture people for personal pleasure. Anybody who would do such a thing would be a horrible person." But at the same time that I say this, I may also be perplexed. Just how is it that I know this, and what exactly makes it true (as I confidently believe it to be)? This, then, would be for me and for most everyone else an instance of theoretical doubt, not personal or existential doubt. For I am not in the least tempted to abandon my belief that torturing people for personal enjoyment is wrong, even while I might have some unresolved theoretical perplexities associated with this belief.

Similarly, I could be puzzling over features of the doctrine of the Trinity (how is it that three persons can be so united that there is one God?) or the doctrine of the incarnation (how is it that Jesus is the Son of God, both truly human and truly divine?). In seriously reflecting about these matters, I may be seeking clarification about important beliefs that are at the same time confidently held, though in many ways still perplexing or mysterious. This too would be a case of theoretical doubt — much puzzlement but no agony of soul and no temptation to jump ship. As a general phenomenon, this is not at all unusual, nor irrational. Both philosophers and physicists find themselves in this situation and do not fault themselves for it.

Theoretical doubt is, clearly, far removed from the dark night of the soul that John Crowe Ransom captures and that will be our concern. It is important to keep these two senses of doubt distinct. "Living with the questions" is not the same as living with the darkness and the sense of Absence. The former can actually be a lot of fun for those who enjoy puzzling and questioning, but there is no fun in the latter — perhaps ultimately spiritual profit, but no fun. Moreover, not everyone who is wrestling with the doctrine of the Trinity or critically reflecting on certain arguments for the existence of God is experiencing existential doubt. After all, some Christians do this for a living, and their Christian faith is not constantly hanging in the balance. It all depends, of course, on the person and the particular circumstances. What is purely an exercise in theoretical doubt for one person may be a case of existential doubt for another.

I have, for example, been in a classroom discussing with students some conceptual and logical challenges to the traditional doctrine of the Trinity. During one such discussion, one particular student who was intently and conscientiously following the discussion became deeply upset to discover that such problems even exist, that Sunday school explanations are not fully adequate (and sometimes not fully orthodox), and that solutions are not easy to come by. One has to work hard at it if helpful progress is to be made — but it can be made, even if mystery remains. This classroom discussion precipitated a minor crisis of faith for this student. If prolonged, requiring more than a brief period of adjustment to these new theological realities, it might even have become existential doubt. So what was for me and many others in the class merely a case of theoretical questioning, though an important bit of questioning, was for this student much more than that. Many Christians, when confronting for the first time theoretical problems associated with their Christian faith, find this unsettling, much like this student who was troubled by complexities associated with the doctrine of the Trinity. They may be assuming that for a belief to be confidently and rationally held it must either be virtually free of theoretical problems or beset by problems that avail themselves of quick and easy responses. But this is not the case for almost all beliefs that we hold, including our most basic and commonsense beliefs. A good introductory course in philosophy will be quick to disabuse one of the notion that serious skeptical challenges are limited to belief in God and objective moral standards. In point of fact, when it comes to exploring the nature and existence of God, we should expect to find puzzles and perplexities. Indeed, if physicists in exploring the nature of matter or light confront puzzles, how much more should we expect to confront puzzles when exploring not the mere subject matter of physics but the nature and reality of an infinite God. Should there be no serious intellectual perplexity, everything falling neatly into place, then we might very well conclude that we are not dealing with God, or at best we are doing so in a superficial way.

Clearly, in their pure forms existential doubt and theoretical doubt are different phenomena. Either one can occur without the other. I can wrestle with faith-generated perplexities and do so without any loss of confidence in the truth of what I believe. I can also be free of such perplexity, having no personal history of dealing with such matters, and suddenly find myself bereft of confidence in God's reality and the truth of the Christian gospel. It may simply descend on a person. In such cases doubt is not the product of a particular intellectual problem or set of problems. It is not: "If only I could make sense of the doctrine of the Trinity, then all would be well." Rather, it is more like this: "When I pray I think I'm just talking to myself. I go to church, but I seem to just be going through the motions. God doesn't seem real to me." Thus it is evident that existential doubt is not the exclusive domain of the skeptically inclined Christian intellectual. It is no respecter of persons. It can happen to any of us. No doubt it has or it will.

QUESTIONS FOR REFLECTION

1. Have you experienced *theoretical* doubt or puzzlement about your Christian faith? Can you give examples of this?

2. Have *theoretical* questions about your Christian beliefs ever led to *existential* uncertainty? If so, how was this resolved? Or has it been?

3. Could it be that those who are greatly disturbed by puzzles and questions about their Christian faith fail to see that such puzzles and questions also attach — if we think about it enough, which we usually don't — to almost all of our most basic beliefs? Could you provide convincing examples of this?

4. Have you ever helped anyone struggling with deep doubt? If so, what did you say or do? Did it prove helpful?

2

Why Truth Matters

Why Relativism Won't Help

Why It's Important to Doubt in the Right Way

When doubters wonder whether their belief that God exists is true or not, they are wondering whether or not there is a divine reality "out there" that corresponds to their belief. They assume, like the rest of us, that the proposition "God exists" is rendered true by the fact that God exists. Simple enough, one might naturally suppose. Indeed, it might seem so simple and so obvious that it's hardly worth mentioning. In point of fact, though, this notion of truth is not accepted in all circles. Admittedly, these are rarefied academic circles. Outside those circles this view of truth is assumed by almost everyone. It is the commonsense view, and to be sure, it's not without its able defenders within the academy, the only place where it needs defenders. Significantly, the charge has been made that this very view of truth is the cause of the doubts and uncertainties that many religious believers experience.[1] The alleged culprit is this correspondence theory of truth. According to this theory, statements seek to describe the way things are, and those statements will be true or false depending on whether matters are the way the statements say they are. Thus, "The cat is on the mat," to use the shopworn example, is true just in case the cat is actually on the mat. So when I wonder whether there is a God or not, I am wondering whether my belief corresponds to the way things are, wondering whether or not there is a divine reality that corresponds to my belief and renders that belief true. Conversely, when I am free of such doubt, I am confident that there is an appropriate correspondence between what I believe and the way things are.

But how can a theory of truth corrupt the church, especially a theory that has been held (at least implicitly) by almost everyone, past and present? It is not after all a theory that has just burst onto the scene. If it has been corrupting the church, it has been doing so for centuries. It corrupts, the claim goes, by engendering unnecessary doubt. And how exactly does it do that? According to the correspondence theory of truth, my belief that there is a God is rendered true by an independently existing divine reality that we call God. Right here is the rub, it is said. I then begin to wonder whether there is this independently

1. See Philip D. Kenneson, "There's No Such Thing as Objective Truth and It's a Good Thing," in *Christian Apologetics in the Post Modern World*, ed. Timothy R. Phillips and Dennis L. Okholm (Downers Grove, Ill.: InterVarsity, 1995), pp. 155-70.

existing divine reality or not. I worry about this, have doubts, and experience anxiety over this question. I search for good arguments, wondering whether they are sound or not. I read books on apologetics, praying for evidence of God's reality. We can, it is suggested, rid ourselves of this unnecessary doubt and frantic uncertainty by jettisoning the correspondence theory of truth. We need to think about truth in a different way, and thereby dispel our doubts. And what is this different way of understanding truth that will be helpful to our doubter? Here is the first suggestion that is offered.

Beliefs are *not* to be understood as mental states, which in the case of God would have the content "God exists," but rather are habits of action. Once we see that beliefs are *not* mental states that may or may not correspond to some reality "out there," we are freed from the worry that this all-important correspondence might not hold. Because beliefs are habits of action, we can, in acquiring the right habits, secure our beliefs, with no fretting about the existence of some corresponding reality. In the case of belief in God, my belief would then consist of going to church, worshiping, praying, having devotions, serving others in God's name, etc. Note that these actions becoming habitual *constitutes* my belief, according to this line of reasoning. It is not, as is typically supposed, that I engage in these actions because I believe in God or that engaging in these activities strengthens my belief in God. Rather, my belief is simply my being habituated to engage in a range of religious practices.

This is not at all convincing. Suppose I am wondering whether I have the $2,000 in my checking account sufficient to cover the check I am about to write. If I confidently write that check, I do so because I judge that there is a correspondence between my belief that I have $2,000 in my account and my account actually having the $2,000. My belief, I judge, is an accurate representation of the way things are. I might reasonably check with the bank to put to rest any uncertainty I might have. What I would not do is abandon the correspondence theory of truth, blaming it for my doubt and worry. And if I do confidently write that check, it is because I believe I have the amount needed in my account to cover that check. It is an expression of my belief, but it itself is not my belief. There is of course an intimate connection between belief and action. Beliefs (plus appropriate desires) can prompt action, and action can in turn support belief. Specifically, worship, prayer, devotions, service in God's name, etc., may be expressions of my belief and may also strengthen my belief, rendering it more robust. Nevertheless, beliefs are not to be reduced to patterns of behavior. So, just as I may wonder whether my check can be covered by the funds in my account, so I may wonder whether there is a God to answer my prayers. In neither case can we solve our wondering and doubts by jettisoning the correspondence theory of truth.

Another approach to truth that might seem to relieve doubters of the burden of their doubt — a possibly more convincing approach than the one just examined — is to relativize truth. "You have your truth. I have my truth. All cultures and religions have their truth. So don't fret. Just accept the truth that you have. Conflicting truth claims should not disturb you. All are true." Certainly relativism is in the air in our contemporary culture, especially relativism about religious and ethical truth claims. This embrace of relativism has been largely motivated in recent years by a noble desire to foster tolerance and acceptance of other cultures and religions. Since every such group, according to this way of viewing matters, has its truth and no one's truth is superior to anyone else's truth, it follows that no one is in a position to lord it over others, consigning their beliefs to the trash can of falsehood and error. It also appears — helpfully for doubters — that we can now rest content with our own truth, undisturbed by the fact that other religions or cultures have different beliefs and therefore different truths. We are not forced to choose between these competing truth claims. We need not worry about who has it right; it so happens, after all, that we all have it right. We have no need to defend our truth claims against other groups who apparently disagree with us. We need not spend time and energy criticizing what they believe as a means of securing what we believe. We are relieved of that burden. We can simply rest content with our truth and let others rest content with theirs. We banish doubt and foster tolerance at one and the same time.

It is important to recognize that to relativize truth is not simply to claim that different cultures, religious traditions, and time periods have different *beliefs* about what is true. Rather, it is the claim that they actually have different *truths*. So as you move from one culture to another or from one religious tradition to another or from one historical period to another, it is not merely what is believed to be true that changes but truth itself — truth about the very same matter. Most people, when they think about it, will find such a claim astonishing. Yet at the popular level relativism is often embraced naively because of a confusion. It is mistakenly thought that relativism is the contention that *truth claims* vary from group to group (which of course they do and which nobody denies), not that *truth itself* varies. But it is the latter claim that should give us pause, and it is the latter claim that is being made by the relativist and is sometimes invoked both to dispel the clouds of doubt and to eliminate the vice of intolerance.

Before returning to our main concern, it is worth noting that there is a serious problem with using relativism as a strategy for fostering tolerance, well-meaning though it may be. For the relativist, unfortunately, there can be no ultimately correct answer to the question: Should we tolerate people from other cultures and religions? There is only the answer given by one's own culture, religion, or historical time period, and this answer, whatever it may be, has as much validity as any other, including the most intolerant. According to relativism, matters come down to this: one has a duty to tolerate the moral and religious beliefs and practices of other traditions and cultures if, but only if, one's own culture believes there is such a duty. But if, as is more often than not the case, one's own culture does not believe this, then one has no such duty. As one commentator has put it, "This is hardly to strike a blow for toleration."[2] So in rejecting relativism, one is not rejecting a satisfactory basis for tolerance; nor is one joining the company of the intolerant.

The reason there are multiple truths is that there are multiple realities, according to the claims of relativists, each socially constructed to meet different contingent needs or interests, or constructed because there are different yet equally valid ways of justifying beliefs about the world. Such a view of matters is nicely illustrated by a *New York Times* story entitled "Indian Tribes Creationists Thwart Archeologists" (October 22, 1996).[3] The backdrop of this story is the differing accounts of the prehistoric origin of Native Americans. The standard view is that they crossed the Bering Strait from Asia some 10,000 years ago. This view, archaeologists and anthropologists inform us, is extensively confirmed by a wide variety of data. The contrasting view found in some Native American traditions is that they came from inside the earth after the earth had been prepared for them by supernatural spirits. The *New York Times* article quoted a number of archaeologists and anthropologists who were not prepared to en-

2. Francis Snare, *The Nature of Moral Thinking* (London and New York: Routledge, 1992), p. 145.

3. I owe this example to Paul Boghossian, *Fear of Knowledge* (New York: Oxford University Press, 2006), pp. 1-2.

dorse the superiority of the scientific account over the Native American account. It was said, for example, that the Native American version of prehistory was just as valid as the archaeological account. (One wonders whether the same embrace of equal validity would be extended to six-day creationists. I suspect not.) By extension one could claim equal validity for one's belief in God based on the biblical and Christian tradition of which one is a part. This is our truth, and we need not be disturbed by the truth that others have, be they polytheists, atheists, scientific naturalists, or whatever. We all have truth. So rest content with your truth, undisturbed by doubt and uncertainty. Well, what should we think of all this?

This kind of relativism comes up against the obstinate conviction that there is a way the world is that is not a mere product of our construals, nor is it subject to our human will. Thus, these two differing and incompatible accounts of the origin of Native Americans force us to choose. If Native Americans, one and all, came from Asia via the Bering Strait, then they did not come from a subterranean world of spirits. This is not to deny that the Native American account is filled with deep religious significance and should be respected as such, but it is not an accurate account of prehistory. So either the scientific account is true or it's not true. It cannot be both. We are not free to turn the past into whatever best serves our preferences, interests, or needs (think of Holocaust deniers), nor can we convincingly claim that both of these accounts are true, their truth depending on equally valid justifying frameworks. In contrast, the commonsense view is that there is an objective reality to which our judgments, individual and communal, must conform. For this reason relativism, with its multiple equally valid social constructions of reality (and nothing more), fails the test of common sense. Common sense may not always win the day, nor should it, but it certainly places the burden of proof on those who would affirm theories that go counter to it. And in this particular case our commonsense conviction is universally shared, deeply embedded in how we view the world and difficult, if not impossible, to eliminate from our thinking. Consequently, those who would challenge it have their work cut out for them, and then some.

So according to our commonsense conviction, it is either the case that God exists or it's not the case that God exists. A person may be unsure which is true, but only one of these propositions can be true; the other of necessity must be false. This is simply a point of logic, and doubters are quite sensibly wondering which one of the two propositions is true. In contrast, talk of religious relativism strikes our doubters as manifestly unhelpful. After all, they belong to a religious tradition that does believe in the existence of God, but their membership doesn't settle matters for them. They doubt all the same and wonder whether their religious tradition is correct in what it believes. Thus they are not confined to that tradition but have the ability to step back from it and critically reflect on its truth claims. This is just what they are doing, and they are wondering, wherein lies the truth? They are attempting to make a determination in this matter, and an embrace of relativism will not provide them with a satisfactory answer or secure any relief from the doubts and uncertainties they have.

Finally and crucially, a relativistic religious vision is incapable of assigning to our belief in God the significance that believers, hopers, seekers, and doubters all see attaching to it. It is a religiously feeble view. In our doubter's eyes the relativist's god (a lowercase *g* seems appropriate here) does not seem to be a god worth having, nor therefore one whose possible loss would prove particularly worrisome, being but one social construction among many, no better and no worse than, say, the atheist's construal. Indeed, if such radical relativism were true, the religious impulse itself would appear to be futile. For we hunger for God, not a god. Our heart (to echo Saint Augustine) will not rest until it finds its rest in the One in whom all things have their source, support, and end. This is the One from whom and through whom and for whom are all things (see Rom. 11:36). Here is the One worthy of our doubts and worthy of our best efforts to confront those doubts. All who struggle with doubt in this way, struggle in the right way.

QUESTIONS FOR REFLECTION

1. How do you understand religious relativism? Is it wide-spread in our culture? In the church? In your church?

2. Are there areas in our religious life, beliefs, or practices where you might correctly say, "Yes, this is relative," but other areas where you might correctly say, "No, this is not relative"? Can you give examples of each?

3. When you examine your own doubt, is that doubt, in the author's words, "the right kind of doubt"? If not, what kind of doubt is it?

3

Why Doubt Should Be Expected

Why Doubt Speaks Well of You

Why the Nonreligious Also Doubt

I t is too strong to claim, as the theologian Paul Tillich did,[1] that doubt is a necessary element of genuine faith, as if you could not possibly have the one without the other. To the contrary, nothing about the concept of faith logically requires doubt, either as an episode occurring at some point in one's journey of faith or as a reality hovering constantly in the background. Nevertheless, if we understand faith as Paul Tillich proposes, doubt should perhaps be expected in the lives of many, possibly most, Christians. Even if it is not a matter of necessity, as Tillich argues, at the very least we should not be surprised by its occurrence. Certainly there are people of genuine Christian faith whom we have good reason to believe have never experienced serious, prolonged doubt. So it can't be a matter

1. Paul Tillich, *Dynamics of Faith* (New York: Harper, 1957), pp. 18-25.

of necessity that they do so. Nevertheless, doubt may be something that should, on the whole, be expected rather than viewed as a kind of spiritual leprosy, both terrible and rare. Few things are more dangerous for the Christian life than the belief that good Christians, doing all the things that good Christians are supposed to do, will never experience prolonged, disturbing doubt. For if we believe that we are one of the few Christians who doubt, then we will tend to see our doubt as being far worse than it really is. This is not to minimize its seriousness unduly. Nevertheless, when we see it as something that has been shared by others, including some of the very best of our number, then we will be able to begin to put it in perspective, to put it in its place, so to speak. Let me explain why I think doubt should be expected (if not necessitated), by using Tillich's notion of faith.

Tillich calls faith "ultimate concern," and he understands ultimate concern as:

1. that which means most to you;
2. that which gives meaning to your life;
3. that which you are willing to sacrifice everything else for.[2]

So understood, it would seem that everyone, secular as well as religious, is a "person of faith," for all of us have some ultimate concern or other. Admittedly this is an id-

2. Tillich, *Dynamics of Faith*, pp. 1-9.

iosyncratic use of the term "faith," but nothing much hinges on it. The point Tillich is making can be made equally well without even using the term. For what is crucial is his observation that all of us have an ultimate concern, no matter how we label it. My ultimate concern could be God, but it could also be my family, my nation, my job, my personal welfare, or any number of things. The object of the genuine Christian's faith, and therefore his or her ultimate concern, is the God and Father of Jesus Christ. In other words, nothing is more important, nothing is more fundamental for thought, values, and behavior. It is what we have built our life around, sacrificed for, defended, sought to further, shared with others. It is what has provided inspiration and motivation, consolation and comfort. And it's just because it is so important, so ultimate in our frame of reference, that we will quite understandably experience serious doubt at least at some point in time. And when it does come, be well advised, it comes with a bang. On the other hand, if the God and Father of Jesus Christ were for us only a peripheral or secondary concern, we would be much less likely to experience any serious, disturbing doubt. What is peripheral in one's life is simply not that important, nor is its loss a particularly disturbing prospect. This would in fact suggest that nominal Christians, those whose church connection is on par with membership in, say, the Rotary Club, will experience no existential doubt. Neither for the nominal Christian nor for the Rotarian will there be the dark night of the soul. So while we certainly do not want to assume that those who are doubt-free are merely nominal Christians, it does make sense to think that those for whom faith is central or ultimate in their lives are more likely to experience distress at the prospect of its loss than those for whom it is merely a peripheral concern. The latter's doubts may lie elsewhere.

The point I'm trying to make can be illustrated in the following somewhat prosaic way. Suppose I am asked to walk two feet above the ground on a wobbly rope bridge that experts on wobbly rope bridges assure me is perfectly safe. I have no problem and no fear as I put that bridge to the test. In other words, I have no doubts. If the bridge should fail, I will simply tumble (if that) to the ground unhurt. There is nothing much at stake, and so nothing much to worry about. But suppose that same bridge, which experts in such matters assure me is perfectly safe, is suspended across the Grand Canyon, and I am once more invited to walk across it. Here there will be doubts aplenty because now everything, indeed my very life, depends on the safety of that bridge. What generates different levels of concern is having so much depend on the safety of the one bridge and so very little on the safety of the other, although the safety of each is equally well assured. More generally, the difference between a peripheral concern and an ultimate concern is, as in the case of these bridges, that so little is at stake in the one case and so much in the other. How much is at stake depends on how important we take an object of concern to be, and this is a very personal matter. With an ultimate concern, one is not only more prone to question but also more likely to have agony of soul even in contemplating the question. Therefore, agony in such circumstances, from a Christian perspective, speaks well of you. You care about all of this. It is important. It matters to you. Maybe this is the price one pays for caring deeply about Christian things, about the God who comes to us in Jesus Christ. But if Tillich is right, *everyone,* Christian or not, pays this price since everyone has an ultimate concern. And ultimate concerns of whatever kind tend at some point to generate doubt.

What is important to note here is that to give up one's Christian faith is not automatically to receive a free pass from serious and unpleasant doubt. Think of men who have poured all their energies into their jobs, sacrificing family and much else on the altar of career success. Such a "faith" will not be impervious to serious second thoughts: "Has this been the wisest and best way to lead my life?" Or consider the woman who has given up everything for her family, including all career prospects and any serious interests outside the home. Confronting an empty nest, she too may wonder about her "faith." Or consider the altruist who has invested all her life in helping others, devoting herself to one humanitarian project after another. She may come to wonder whether she should have given more time and energy to her own personal projects (and perhaps family goals). Even the individual who has sought a balanced life, avoiding what might be considered an overemphasis in any one area, becoming in other words a person who appears to lack a "faith" in Tillich's sense, may also ponder and doubt. "Have I sunk into a kind of mediocrity, having no overriding passion to guide my life, to give my life a deep controlling purpose and to help me secure some significant achievements?" Doubt, it would appear, is ubiquitous. Unquestionably there are a lot of doubters in this world of ours, most of them not religious. They are all wrestling with what a good and satisfying life should look like, and they are experiencing uncertainty about the lives they have chosen to live, even in cases where we might judge the choice to be an admirable one.

There is, of course, a difference between our religious doubter and our other doubters. The religious doubter is uncertain about the *existence* of God, but the other doubters are not uncertain about the existence of their jobs, their families, or their philanthropic projects. It is the *value* of these activities and the central place they have been given in their lives that they question, not the existence of the activities themselves. Nevertheless, religious doubters, to point out but one parallel with these other doubters, may, amidst their doubts, wonder whether the *possibility* of God, in contrast to their former *certainty* of God, is worth continued faithfulness, worth the central place it has heretofore been given in their lives. "How am I now," they wonder, "to live my life? Should I reorient my priorities? Should the *possibility* of God command the same loyalty and commitment as the *certainty* of God?" What does it mean to be true to a possibility? So they struggle. This is the same kind of struggle that our other doubters are experiencing. They too are wondering where their central commitment should be. To be sure, our Christian doubters also wonder about the existence of God. In this regard they do differ. Nevertheless, their doubt, both its presence and its seriousness, shares a crucial feature common to all existential doubt. For them it is a faith that has been directed at the God they have deeply believed comes to them in Jesus Christ. And now, they wonder, where do I go from here?

In other words, even if one were to abandon all metaphysical claims about a transcendent reality and embrace a naturalistic worldview, doubts may still not be eliminated. Naturalists too can be doubters. They are not members of a doubt-free community. "Possibly I am missing out on something vitally significant about the universe and my place in it. Perhaps matters are not quite as clear as I have thought, not so obvious that there is no God. Perhaps I have been too quick to dismiss all religious claims. Just maybe there is a God." Of course, it's possible that one may not doubt any of this. If we are here dealing with *tendencies* rather than *necessities,* as I have suggested (qualifying Tillich), one may go into the grave without much by way of disturbing doubt. But it is not likely. Most people, no matter their ultimate concern, will at some point experience some doubt, possibly severe doubt. So keep this in mind, Christian doubter: you are a member of a far bigger club than you might have imagined. Its membership includes the religious and nonreligious, young and old, you and me. At least you are struggling and doubting where the stakes couldn't be any higher and where the truth (wherever it lies) couldn't be any more important. Why exchange this doubt and this struggle for some other where the significance, hopes, and possibilities are so much less?

I recall hearing an impressive chapel talk by a colleague of mine entitled "Choosing Your Mysteries." Mysteries, she said, cannot be avoided. They are simply a fact of life. No matter what vision of human existence you embrace, you will, if you are at all thoughtful and honest, encounter mystery. Therefore, my colleague concluded, do not hesitate to choose this mystery: we come to the Father, through the Son and by the Spirit. Maybe another sermon could be preached entitled "Choosing Your Doubts." So fated to doubt, as perhaps some of us are, let's stake out that terrain where we choose to have our doubts and our struggles. And what better place than where we find ourselves right now.

<hr>

QUESTIONS FOR REFLECTION

1. Is it reasonable to believe that the more time, money, energy, and emotions you put into something and the more you sacrifice for it, the more likely you are, at some point, to have doubt about what you are doing or believing? But doesn't such strong personal investment

also render that commitment more robust and confident? Could both be true? Can you speak to this from
personal experience?

2. *Prior* to becoming Christians some individuals experience severe doubt, indeed existential doubt, about
their manner of life, its goals and purposes. Is this true
of you or anybody you have known?

3. Has your own faith been built around the "certainty of
God" and/or the "possibility of God"? How important
should the *possibility* of God be for structuring a life of
faith? Should the "possibility of God" prompt strong
commitment? Should it differ from commitment on the
basis of the "certainty of God"?

4

Why Doubt Hits Hardest When It's First Experienced

Why It's Crucial to See Yourself as a Believer Who Is Tempted to Doubt, Not a Doubter Who Is Tempted to Believe

I begin with a personal story. It was during my first year in seminary, of all places, that deeply disturbing and pervasive doubt, not just theoretical puzzling, possessed me for the first time. Here I was in seminary preparing for the ministry in some form or other: the pastoral ministry or possibly teaching (as it turned out to be). I was charting the future direction of my life based on beliefs that I now felt very uncertain about. Before this I had been so confident, so very sure. Now there were doubt and uncertainty, and an emptiness. What a contrast! Up to that point I had never seriously entertained the possibility that I could be mistaken about what I believed and what I had committed myself to. It was always a logical possibility of course, like it's a logical possibility that the United States is now at war with Canada, but it was not a real possibility that I could even begin to take seriously. So what had been only a logical possibility now became in my mind a real possibility. I could very well be mistaken. Interestingly, my doubt was not the product of wrestling with critical accounts of the historicity of the Old and New Testaments, nor a product of skeptical challenges to arguments for the existence of God, nor the product of conceptual difficulties related to the doctrines of the Trinity, the incarnation, and such like. These may bring on doubt for others, but it was not so for me, at least not on that occasion. In fact, I was not deeply concerned with any of these issues at the time. It was an uncertainty that simply descended upon me for no obvious reason. This seems very much in line with what Roland Bainton, the church historian, observed when discussing the faith struggles experienced by Martin Luther: "The very nature of the dark night of the soul is that it may be induced by nothing at all."[1] So it seems to have been with me.

I had come to Christian faith in high school. To be sure, much innocence is associated with teenage Christianity, and no doubt I shared fully in that innocence. After all, the capacity for theological sophistication and serious philosophical reflection at such an age is quite limited. In addition, there is a shortage of life experience. So certainly there was much I did not know or under-

1. Roland Bainton, "Luther's Struggle for Faith," in *The Reformation: Basic Interpretations*, ed. Lewis W. Spitz (Lexington, Mass.: Heath, 1972), p. 203.

stand. Nevertheless, as I now look back on my entry into the Christian faith, with whatever theological understanding and life experience I have since acquired, I have no complaints to register, but only deep gratitude for the message and the messengers who were instrumental in bringing me to faith. It was the story — the old, old story of God's love and forgiveness freely extended in Jesus Christ. There was a quiet but deep emotional component to it, but no emotionalism produced by singing, clapping of hands, and intense preaching. I raise no objections to any of these because they too can be a context for a genuine encounter with Christ. I only observe that my experience was not of that kind. Quite the contrary, I launched forth on my journey of faith in a context that was, if anything, rather sober and cerebral — a verse-by-verse examination of the book of Romans in a small-group Bible study. To this day I consider myself a convert of the apostle Paul. The very words that the apostle wrote to the Christian church in Rome so many centuries earlier became the medium through which faith in Christ was evoked in me, a twentieth-century American teenager. Amazing, when you think of it. The original recipients of that letter lived in a far different culture, almost two millennia removed from the time I walk the planet. Yet the same transforming message reached us both. To be sure, there was much in this theologically daunting letter that I did not understand (nor do I to this day), but I did understand enough for it to bring me to the point of Christian commitment. So I can say that my conversion had at least one thing in common with that of the great Saint Augustine — the pivotal role played by the book of Romans. The Christian gospel communicated to me during this Bible study was in no way aberrant or in need of subsequent revision. So, looking back on my initial response of faith, I have no reason to feel that I was emotionally manipulated or theologically misled. Where people subsequently do have such negative reactions, there can be an accompanying hostility toward the Christian message and its messengers. Such hostility is something quite different, however, from existential doubt, where the problem is not anger that needs somehow or other to be worked through. Rather, it is doubt about what you want to be true, something you cherish and care deeply about. There is, after all, a big difference between a belligerent and enthusiastic doubt, on the one hand, and a reluctant and painful doubt, on the other. Mine was in the latter category, and this is just what is meant by existential doubt.

It was with much joy and certainty that I launched forth on my faith journey. This confidence continued through college, a time when, for many others, serious doubt strikes for the first time. In contrast, my collegiate years were a time of zealous sharing of a faith confidently held. There was no doubt. None at all. I actually found it stimulating, even enjoyable, puzzling over various issues raised by my new faith, such puzzling being for me nothing more than theoretical doubt. In my case, *existential* doubt arrived during my first semester in seminary when I would have least expected it. And when it came, it came with a vengeance. There were sleepless nights and agony of soul. For whatever reason, serious existential doubt hits hardest and hurts most when we experience it for the first time. It will, if I can generalize from my own experience, never be quite that bad again. This, for first-timers, should be of some consolation. Further, it makes sense that it be so. Never before having experienced such doubt, it was impossible in advance to even imagine what it would be like. Moreover, you may have been told that Christians with God's Spirit as an indwelling presence do not experience doubt, but here you are experiencing just such doubt and in spades. When it comes, you feel totally isolated, as if you are experiencing what no other Christian has ever experienced. There is no one to talk to, or so you believe. For doubt has not been a topic of conversation in Christian circles as far as you are aware, and that prompts you to conclude that there are no other doubters, no one you can talk with who would truly understand. This is an especially critical time in a person's journey of faith. For if this first experience of existential doubt can be survived, so can any subsequent episode. It is here that a person stands most in need of wise counsel and some helpful strategies for responding to this newly experienced, soul-disturbing doubt. Be well assured, existential doubt can be survived with faith fully intact. Many thoughtful and spiritually serious Christians can testify to such survival. They lived to tell the tale. But it is, all the same, a difficult and challenging time.

During this period of my life I found myself wrestling

with the following question: Am I or am I not a believer? Am I or am I not a Christian? Could it be, I thought to myself, that I am only 49 percent a believer but 51 percent a doubter, and therefore not really a believer at all? But then again, maybe I am 51 percent a believer and only 49 percent a doubter. Of course, we can't slice matters quite so finely, and I'm not suggesting that we can. The point is that matters for me seemed too close to call. Is my dominant state of heart and mind belief and confidence or doubt and uncertainty? Which is it? This question was deeply disturbing. I was as much concerned with what I was, believer or doubter, as I was concerned with where God was. I wrestled with this question almost to the point of exhaustion, but I was unable to determine which was the case. I introspected and introspected but could not make a determination. What I needed, of course, was someone to tell me that this was not the time to decide this matter nor the right way to go about it. But I had no such wise counsel.

I might note that the uncertainty over my status as a believer may have been the product of confusion. I may have mistakenly thought that belief is incompatible with uncertainty. But, of course, it is not. To have a belief — in God's existence or in anything else for that matter — it is only necessary to hold that one's belief is more likely true than false. Belief is compatible, then, with varying degrees of uncertainty. Had I been asked, "Do you think your religious beliefs are more likely true than false?" I might have responded with a "yes." In which case I would have been a believer, just not a very confident one. But then again I might have responded, "I just don't know," in which case my status as a believer would have been questionable. And that was exactly my worry at the time, whether my uncertainty was a product of a confusion or not. And I found this worry disturbing and persistent.

Somehow or other this had to stop. So I declared to myself, in an act of self-characterization, "I am a believer who is tempted to doubt; I am not a doubter who is tempted to believe. What is important about me is my belief, not my doubt." Admittedly this was an act of will. I simply declared it to be so. And to a considerable extent you do become what you characterize yourself as being. Certainly there are limits to this, indeed vast limits, but for me, at least in this context, it worked, and things began to settle down and take on a more normal character. This is not to say that doubt was forever banished, for it was not. But doubt was put in its place. And it is important to do just that, put doubt in its place, which means not to let it rule and reign in your life. It may be there — we need not deny its presence or pretend it's not real — but we need not let it control our lives either. I realized that although doubt is an aspect of who I am, it is not by any means all that I am. There are other important features about me that I need to fully acknowledge. For example, I desire God's strong presence in my life. I do love God. I do believe that God has spoken to me through Scripture and in worship, and that I have communed with God in prayer. To be sure, I was wondering about this and experiencing doubts, but there was, after all, something there to be doubted, and what was doubted was as real and as much a part of me as the doubt itself. It was that very part of me that I affirmed. I was, I decided, a believer with doubts.

One can also make a different decision. One can decide in favor of doubt rather than in favor of what is doubted. That too would be an act of will, an act of self-characterization. One can do this simply by turning away from the life of faith — the church, prayer, Christian fellowship, Scripture, service in the name of Christ. By such actions one in essence declares that one has ceased to be a believer in what one formerly held dear. One decides no longer to do what believers do. In those circumstances one is not so much being overcome by doubt, as people sometimes like to put it, as one is *deciding* in favor of doubt. I may not be responsible for my doubts, but I am responsible for my response to my doubts. To speak of being "overcome" by doubt is to portray oneself as a hapless victim when in fact what may be moving one away from the Christian faith is a decision, maybe not always a fully conscious one, to favor doubt over belief, to construe oneself as a doubter rather than as a believer and to act accordingly, when a very different construal and a very different pattern of behavior were equally open to one. But that was not, thankfully, the decision I made. It may have been — I cannot say for sure — that my decision did not so much create the reality as it revealed what was there all along, a believer with doubts. It was, in any case, a crucial move in my personal struggle. In brief, that is my story, but there is another story and another more powerful witness to faith who amidst his struggles also chose to construe matters in favor of faith.

Dietrich Bonhoeffer was a pastor-theologian who was imprisoned and ultimately executed for his involvement in a plot to overthrow Hitler and the Nazi regime. He was one of those rare individuals who was both a thinker and a doer. He was capable of profound theological thought, and his writings endure to this day and have enriched and inspired many. Yet he was also capable of courageous action, risking and ultimately sacrificing his life by opposing the evils of Nazism. As with his writings, so has his life proved an enduring legacy. When in prison, cut off from family, friends, and fiancée, facing an uncertain future, he confronted severe challenges to his faith that few, if any, of us will ever experience. He too, understandably, had his dark times. While in prison he wrote these words:

Who Am I?

Who am I? They often tell me
I would step from my cell's confinement
Calmly, cheerfully, firmly,
Like a squire from his country-house.

Who am I? They often tell me
I would talk to my warders
freely and friendly and clearly,
as though it were mine to command.

Who am I? They tell me
I would bear the days of misfortune
equably, smiling, proudly,
like one accustomed to win.

Am I then really all that which other men tell of?
Or am I only what I know of myself,
restless and longing and sick, like a bird in a cage,
struggling for breath, as though hands were
        compressing my throat,
yearning for colours, for flowers, for the voices
        of birds,
thirsting for words of kindness, for neighborliness,
trembling with anger at despotisms and petty
        humiliation,
tossing in expectation of great events,
powerlessly trembling for friends at an infinite
        distance,
weary and empty at praying, at thinking, at making,
faint, and ready to say farewell to it all?

Who am I? This or the other?
Am I one person today, and tomorrow another?
Am I both at once? A hypocrite before others,
And before myself a contemptibly woebegone
        weakling?
Or is something within me still like a beaten army,
Fleeing in disorder from victory already achieved?
Who am I? They mock me, these lonely questions

of mine.

Whoever I am, thou knowest, O God, I am thine.[2]

Who am I? The question may mock us as well. A believer or a doubter? For others a confident example of faith and for ourselves an uncertain woebegone struggler? Who am I? "Whoever I am, thou knowest, O God, I am thine."

———— ∞ ————

QUESTIONS FOR REFLECTION

1. The author describes his first encounter with "existential doubt" and a sense of God's absence. Have you had a comparable experience? If so, what was it like?

2. What might prompt someone who has experienced severe doubt to keep it private? Could a person have good reasons for doing so? Should such disclosures be selective?

3. What do you think it means to put doubt in its place? Have you ever consciously done that?

2. Dietrich Bonhoeffer, *Letters and Papers from Prison*, ed. Eberhard Bethge (New York: Simon and Schuster, 1971), pp. 347-48. Reprinted with the permission of Scribner, a Division of Simon & Schuster, Inc., from *Letters and Papers from Prison, Revised, Enlarged Ed.* by Dietrich Bonhoeffer. Translated from the German by R. H. Fuller, Frank Clark, et al. Copyright © 1953, 1967, 1971 by SCM Press Ltd. All rights reserved.

5

Why a Week with Mother Teresa Might Be Better for the Doubter Than a Week with C. S. Lewis

Often the best response to doubt and a sense of God's absence is Christian service, reaching out to others in their need, and doing so consciously in the name of Christ. If in the midst of our struggles we are given the choice of miraculously going back in time to spend a week with C. S. Lewis or even with the great Thomas Aquinas, confronting and responding to faith's intellectual challenges, or spending a week with Mother Teresa, ministering to the poorest of the poor in the name of Christ on the streets of Calcutta, choose to be with Mother Teresa. The choice would be a hard one, admittedly, but I think it would be the right one. This same point is made by the novelist Flannery O'Connor, who tells how Gerard Manley Hopkins, the poet priest, responded to a request by fellow poet Robert Bridges to tell him how he might, amidst his struggles, come to believe.[1]

1. Flannery O'Connor, *The Habit of Being* (New York: Farrar, Straus and Giroux, 1979), pp. 476-77.

Bridges no doubt expected an extended philosophical and theological response, of which Hopkins, of course, was quite capable. But that was not what Bridges received. Rather, Hopkins responded with just two words: "Give alms." Certainly an intriguing reply. It is in charity, Hopkins suggests, that God is to be found and our spirits revived.

Jesus himself seems to suggest that knowing is connected to doing. "If anyone chooses to do God's will, he will find out whether my teaching comes from God" (John 7:17 NIV). The Christian faith is, after all, not just a set of doctrines to be believed, but a way of life to be entered into, and this way of life involves charity and love. As Flannery O'Connor put it, "Don't get so entangled with intellectual difficulties that you fail to look for God in this way."[2] Indeed, thinking about our faith is important, but acting on our faith is equally important, perhaps even more so during those dark nights in our journey of faith. Crucially, to serve others sacrificially, as one would at the side of Mother Teresa, is to bring one's life into conformity with the character of the God of love that Christians see in Jesus. Just as one might find God in prayer and worship, so one might find God when serving others in the name of the One who is eternal love. It is not only that we would be serving others, but that we would be doing so, in our imaginary case, with one whose life was a beautiful "demonstration of God," to

2. O'Connor, *The Habit of Being,* p. 477.

use a phrase Mother Teresa herself coined in calling Christians to be models of God's love and compassion in this world. We may want a logical demonstration of God's existence, but perhaps even better is a living demonstration of God in the lives of those who love God with all their heart, soul, and mind, and their neighbor as themselves. So we not only serve others, but we serve others with others who with heartfelt concern do so in Christ's name. This may be as good a response to doubt as we can find, seeing God alive and active, working through us and through our fellow laborers.

It might be objected that choosing a week with Mother Teresa over a week with C. S. Lewis is a curious decision, granting as we now know that what is being recommended, service in the name of Christ, did not work for Mother Teresa. Indeed, Mother Teresa herself experienced a prolonged dark night of the soul and agonized over a sense of God's absence, "no longer feeling Jesus' presence," despite her sacrificial service. All this, apparently, to the end of her days. But Mother Teresa's circumstances may be rather special, as we shall see in a later reflection. Despite the darkness, it was when serving the poor that Mother Teresa felt closest to God and had a sense of his presence. "Yet deep down somewhere in my heart that longing for God keeps breaking through the darkness. When outside — in the work — or meeting people — there is a presence — of somebody living very close — in very me. — I don't know what this is — but very often even every day — that love in me for God grows more real. — I find myself telling Jesus unconsciously most strange tokens of love."[3]

A colleague of mine, a professional philosopher who has written and taught in the area of Christian apologetics and is therefore well acquainted with the intellectual give-and-take over the question of God's existence and the truth of the Christian faith, tells of an encounter with severe doubt that he experienced during his college years. In his junior year, this philosophy major was unable to find any arguments for God's existence that in his judgment could withstand critical scrutiny. He was also convinced that the only way he could have a justified confidence in God's reality was to possess at least one such argument, and ideally several. A fully satisfactory argument would be a formal piece of reasoning that had strong premises leading by logical steps to the inescapable conclusion that God exists. But no such argument was forthcoming. The arguments examined simply did not satisfy him. Consequently he was engulfed by deep, depressing doubt. What was at the center of his Christian faith, the very existence of God, was now called into question. Moreover, in the history of philosophy, as he had come to see, the world's best minds had been unable to reach agreement on this issue, unable to resolve matters with arguments found compelling by all. Indeed, the de-

3. *Mother Teresa: Come Be My Light; The Private Writings of the "Saint of Calcutta,"* edited with commentary by Brian Kolodiejchuk, M.C. (New York: Doubleday, 2007), p. 211.

bate continues to this day. Is there a God or isn't there? No definitive answer was forthcoming from the philosophical community, only continued debate and disagreement. How could he, mere philosophical neophyte that he was, expect to come to a determination in this matter? Of course, it's not necessary to have an argument that satisfies everyone — always an impossibility — so long as it satisfies you. But he couldn't find such an argument, and even if he did, it would be held suspect because, as he knew, there would be intelligent persons, philosophers past and philosophers present, who were not convinced.

One may question, however, whether the test of a belief should be its endorsement by the philosophical community. If that were so, one would be hard pressed to find any belief of significance that passed muster. Free will, moral agency, truth, knowledge, an external world, other minds, a continuing self, the trustworthiness of sensory experience, and much more have come under skeptical attack and are the object of continuing philosophical debate. The question of God's existence fares no worse than all the other topics that have been discussed and debated among philosophers over the centuries. These debates and disagreements concern some of the most basic and commonsense beliefs that people hold, beliefs they never would have thought to question. It is also the case, we should keep in mind, that some of the finest minds (philosophers and others) have been convinced by arguments for the existence of God, arguments propounded with a great deal of technical skill and sophistication. My colleague subsequently did come to see that the arguments were better than he had thought, but he also came to see that they were less important than he had thought, less central to his own confidence in God's reality, a confidence that was fully justified apart from those arguments.

What is of special interest for our purposes is that my good friend's faith was revived not by discovering a sound, possibly bulletproof argument for God's existence but by something quite different — participation in a missions trip to Mexico during spring break. On that trip he was involved with several hundred other students in Christian service, evangelism, and worship. This had a profound effect on him. He simply put it this way: "through these experiences I had a strong sense of God's presence and activity."[4] Doubt was dispelled and a confident faith restored. He perceived while serving others that God was working through him and through those with whom he served. But, of course, for that to happen he first had to place himself in God's service, as he did by participating in that missions trip. In other words, he had to "give alms," and he did.

This suggested response finds support in that great epistle of love, First John: "Beloved, let us love one another; for love is of God, and he who loves is born of God and knows God. He who does not love does not know God; for God is love. . . . If we love one another, God

4. James Taylor, *Introducing Apologetics* (Grand Rapids: Baker Academic, 2006), p. 10.

abides in us and his love is perfected in us" (1 John 4:7, 8, 12 RSV). There is a deep, intimate connection between love, on the one hand, and abiding in and knowing God, on the other. The key is "loving one another." To be sure, John has in mind the love we are to have for the brethren, fellow believers. I may, however, be forgiven for extending the object of our love to all human beings, to all for whom Christ died, believers and others. And John is quick to tell us that this love is not merely sentimentality or warm feelings unaccompanied by loving action. It is a more substantial love than that, as he tells us. "But if any one has the world's goods and sees his brother in need, yet closes his heart against him, how does God's love abide in him? Little children, let us not love in word or speech but in deed and in truth" (3:17, 18 RSV). It is love embodied and acted out, the giving of oneself, not feelings without action, that unites us to God. It is caring and compassionate love that reaches out to others in their need. It is love in its fullest, richest sense. It is with this love that God abides in us and we abide in God. However, First John is not a paean of praise to love in the abstract, as if love is God and we have no God but love. Love is not our God. Rather, our *God* is love, and the God of love is the same God who created us, loved us before we loved him, and sent his Son to be "the expiation for our sins" (4:10 RSV). Therefore, we are admonished, "If God so loved us, we also ought to love one another" (4:11 RSV). This is the context that renders theologically sensible the claim that to abide in love is to abide in God.

46

It is more likely, I am suggesting, that God will be found in the course of serving others in the name of Christ than in the course of constructing, even if successfully, good arguments for the existence of God, which is by no means a fruitless activity. In reaching out to others in love, we ourselves are drawn into the orbit of God's love. We begin to see the world's need in the same way a compassionate God sees that need. We bring our will into harmony with God's will. We provide occasion for God to be active in and through us, and we witness God's activity in and through the lives of those with whom we serve and labor. Unamuno, the Spanish philosopher, put matters in very stark terms: "For God goes out to meet him who seeks Him with love and by love, and hides Himself from him who searches for Him with the cold and loveless reason. God wills that the heart should have rest, but not the head, reversing the order of the physical life in which the head sleeps and rests at times while the heart wakes and works unceasingly."[5] Of course, we can love God with our minds, as Jesus himself reminds us (Matt. 22:37), and even our feeble intellectual efforts at constructing arguments for God's existence (some no doubt more robust than others) may be expressive of a heart reaching out to God and can be an act of love. There is no need to deny that. And yet a sophisticated philosophical exercise, highly technical and analytical when done well, and not

5. Miguel de Unamuno, *Tragic Sense of Life* (New York: Dover, 1954), p. 194.

unprofitable for some purposes, may not be all that the heart needs. Something more is needed. So give alms. Yes, spend that week with Mother Teresa. Go on that missions trip.

———— ✺ ————

QUESTIONS FOR REFLECTION

1. Has your faith ever been revived or rendered more confident by meaningful service for others in the name of Christ? Have you seen this in others? What forms might such service best take?

2. For a Christian, what does it mean to abide in love? How would you go about doing this? What sense can you make of the claim that to "abide in love" is to "abide in God"?

6

Why It's Important to Have a Theology of Divine Absence

Why It's Important to Have the Right Theology of Absence

Why C. S. Lewis Can Help Us

One can have a theology of just about anything. Theological reflection can have as its object standard Christian doctrines — for example, the incarnation or the atonement — and much theology does. But theological reflection can also venture further afield by directing its attention to aspects of our *human* experience that we find perplexing — for example, why does God allow all the evil in the world? — or aspects of our *Christian* experience that puzzle us — for example, why doesn't God answer my prayers? These would be theological attempts to make Christian sense out of what doesn't seem to make sense. Those are important questions, but we have another. Why does God seem absent from my life and leave me in this state of doubt and uncertainty? Why is this happening to me?

One theological response to this question is almost a kind of orthodoxy in some circles, namely, that there is something spiritually wrong with you that needs fixing. What is wrong could be any one of a number of things, but it is always something that is wrong with *you*. Maybe it's unconfessed sin that has broken the close, intimate relationship you can have and once did have with God. It is that very relationship, it would be pointed out, that generates the confidence that God is real and banishes doubt, but the relationship has been severed through sin that remains unconfessed and unrepented of. Or maybe this relationship with God is not being nourished through worship, prayer, and a healthy devotional life. No wonder God seems absent. You have simply shut God out of your life. According to this understanding of the matter, what is needed is a diagnosis of your particular problem and then a recommendation for the appropriate cure: repent of that sin or nurture your relationship with God through worship, prayer, and Scripture. Here the doubter or the person struggling with a sense of Absence is viewed as spiritually derelict in some way or other. If it were not for the dereliction, there would be no problem, no existential doubt, no Absence, and no dark night of the soul. Here we have a theology of Absence, a theology of doubt, but it does not ring completely true.

To be sure, such an understanding of matters has captured something vitally important for the Christian life. Indeed, sin should be repented of and the means of grace employed faithfully. These are reminders that we all need to hear and act on. But an approach to Absence and existential doubt that blames the doubter has its focus on something other than the problem we are addressing. One may, let us suppose, be drifting in one's Christian life, indifferent to the means of grace, charmed and attracted to what is incompatible with one's Christian calling, and so forth. This is anything but the dark night of the soul. In contrast, when experiencing existential doubt or a sense of Absence, one is not indifferent to Christian things. On the contrary, one cares deeply about them. It's not (or at least in most cases it's not) that worship, prayer, and Scripture are not active parts of one's life. These practices most likely were quite central and heartfelt when the dark night descended and may have continued being so. This is not a case of spiritual indifference. The agony of soul indicates how much one cares. It's because one deeply cares that the presence of doubt and Absence is so painful. There is likely as much and maybe more concern for spiritual matters in the mind and heart of the doubter and struggler than there is in the mind and heart of the one who offers a little too easily the advice to repent and start reading one's Bible. In fact, the one offering such advice doesn't seem to fully understand the problem and therefore is not in a good position to help. There is a time and a place for such advice, but not here. It may actually make matters worse. What is needed is a better theology.

It is here that reflections by C. S. Lewis may help us understand this dark matter. Lewis offers us, in essence, a theology of Absence in the pages of his deservedly famous *Screwtape Letters.*[1] In this book Screwtape, the senior demon and uncle of Wormwood, a junior demon, instructs his nephew through a series of letters in the art of attacking Christians spiritually. In the course of one such letter, Lewis through Screwtape offers us a theological understanding of why there are these times of Absence. Wormwood, a novice in these matters, thinks all is going well in his assault on one Christian believer who has been put under his "care" and whose "religious phase is dying away." Wormwood thinks this is his doing, but he is mistaken. This is not Wormwood's doing at all, but is a natural and to-be-expected phenomenon. It is what Lewis calls the "law of undulation." In every area of life we experience "troughs and peaks." We have times of richness, confidence, emotional robustness (peaks) from which we fall back, where matters seem less real, less rich, and where we are less confident (troughs). Being human, we undulate (fluctuate, rise and fall) not only in our spiritual life but also in every significant aspect of our life. Think of marriage, of our commitment to some charitable cause, pursuing an education, going to work everyday — peaks and troughs. So Screwtape tells Wormwood, don't for a moment think this is your doing. It's not. It is simply part of their humanity. And certainly when we, whose Christian experience began at a peak, experience a trough for the first time, it can be devastating. Lewis is pointing out

1. C. S. Lewis, *The Screwtape Letters* (New York: Macmillan, 1957), pp. 44-52.

that this is merely the law of undulation at work, even if it is our first experience of it. These troughs may not always be agonizing dark nights of the soul; they may merely be an absence of zest and enthusiasm, a kind of dullness of spirit. This is by no means unique to the spiritual life. In all our commitments we go through these undulations. This is not a result of spiritual or moral dereliction, but a fact about our basic humanity.

Certainly if one is to live a successful life, one must come to terms with this reality. To quit or cease to be faithful once one enters a trough is a sure and certain prescription for failure in all those good and noble tasks that our lives are hopefully committed to. To have constancy in life's projects requires that we remain faithful in the troughs as well as on the peaks. And it is helpful to recognize that this challenge confronts us in every important aspect of our lives. We must not be innocents, expecting that in all matters worthy of our best energy and deepest commitment there will be only peaks. Such innocence, if we do not mature beyond it, will ultimately bring disillusionment and failure. I cannot help but think of students who begin a new semester with zeal and enthusiasm. They are focused, and they are disciplined. They are eager to learn. This continues for a few weeks. At this point in the semester they are experiencing an educational peak. But as the semester wears on the excitement abates, matters become routine, difficult material they need to master lacks immediate interest (but not long-term value), and their spirits begin to flag. They are entering a trough. This is true for all students, not just for some. It is the law of undulation at work. The students who obtain a real education are not those who have only peaks (such students don't exist) but those who persist faithfully through the troughs. It's how you handle the troughs, not whether you encounter them, that determines the educational outcome. As in the educational life, so also in the spiritual life — peaks and troughs. So don't be surprised by their occurrence, just be faithful.

Then Lewis, through Screwtape, makes a further observation that may strike some readers as startling but is most germane to our present concerns. He argues that this loss of a strong-felt divine presence is *God's doing*. It is not the result of any failing on the part of the Christian, nor the result of the activity of dark forces. Wormwood gets no credit. It's God's doing. It's an act of divine withdrawal. Screwtape observes that God, in dealing with new Christians, "is prepared to do a little overriding at the beginning. He will set them off with communications of His presence which, though faint, seem great to them, with emotional sweetness, and easy conquest over temptation. But He never allows this state of affairs to last long. Sooner or later He withdraws, if not in fact, at least from their conscious experience, all those supports and incentives."[2] But, we may wonder, why wouldn't God allow this state of affairs to last long, indeed to last forever? Why not continue to sweep us along with the strong sense of his

2. Lewis, *The Screwtape Letters*, pp. 46-47.

mighty presence, so that there are only peaks, no troughs, only unwavering confidence uninterrupted by periods when God seems remote and absent, and matters are doubtful?

This is because, Lewis suggests, God does not want to override the human will. To sweep us along in this way would do just that. God wants us to freely walk with him, not to carry us along by a perpetual flood of good feelings and strong emotions. We are not to be like the moth irresistibly drawn to the light or like metal pulled inexorably to the magnet (my analogies) because God, as Lewis puts it, wants to "woo," not to "ravish." So God "withdraws," not himself of course, but that strong sense of his presence. "He leaves the creature to stand upon its own legs — to carry out from the will alone duties which have lost all relish. . . . He wants them to learn to walk and must therefore take away His hand; and if only the will to walk is really there He is pleased even with their stumbles."[3] Are we willing (if willing it is) to be faithful only when buoyed by the good feelings and absolute confidence of an overwhelming presence? It's easy to be faithful and true then. Who wouldn't be? But if I am overwhelmed by a divine presence, then in some sense I am not giving myself to God so much as I am being taken, "ravished," "absorbed." Thus the price of freedom is a certain felt distance from God. George MacDonald, who greatly influenced Lewis and was greatly admired by Lewis, put matters this way:

3. Lewis, *The Screwtape Letters*, p. 47.

"God does not, by the instant gift of His Spirit, make us always feel right, deserve good, love purity, aspire after Him and His will. . . . The truth is this: He wants to make us in His own image, choosing the good, *refusing* the evil. How could He effect this if He were always moving us from within, as He does at divine intervals toward the beauty of holiness?"[4]

Screwtape goes on to warn Wormwood: "Do not be deceived. . . . Our cause is never more in danger than when a human, no longer desiring, but still intending, to do our Enemy's will, looks round upon a universe from which every trace of Him seems to have vanished, and asks why he has been forsaken, and still obeys."[5] The reason Screwtape's cause is in danger is that God uses the trough periods more than the peak periods to shape Christians into the kind of beings he wants them to become. Lewis does not elaborate. It might be suggested that we will need to draw upon all — every ounce — of our love and desire for God in order to be faithful during these dark and doubtful times, and this love and desire will in turn be further strengthened and deepened by that faithfulness. In contrast, "So long as we have nothing to say to God, nothing to do with Him, save in the sunshine of the mind when we feel Him near us, we are," as MacDonald concludes, "poor creatures, willed upon, not willing."[6]

4. *George MacDonald: An Anthology*, ed. C. S. Lewis (New York: Macmillan, 1947), pp. 17-18.

5. Lewis, *The Screwtape Letters*, p. 47.

6. *George MacDonald*, p. 17.

So Lewis has made two suggestions for why we go through these hard times of doubt and dryness, one natural, the law of undulation, and one supernatural, divine withdrawal. We can use these suggestions to better understand these hard times. The suggestion that this is a natural part of our being human and/or a divine strategy for enabling us to walk freely with God may help us make sense of our situation consistent with the reality of a God who deeply cares for us. Thus Lewis's observations serve a certain apologetical role, helping us respond to the charge that a loving God would not allow such dark and threatening times to come into the lives of those who love him and who are the object of his love. But to the contrary, perhaps God would do just that, and perhaps for the reasons given and further developed by John of the Cross (as we shall see in our next set of reflections). This understanding will hopefully render those dark periods, if not less painful, at least less perplexing and therefore possibly more bearable, pain and all. Moreover, looking back on these troubled times of doubt, though now inhabiting sunnier climes, we may want some theological understanding of what has transpired in our lives. In addition to preparing us to deal with any future recurrences in our own lives, a theology of Absence may assist us in helping others who are undergoing similar challenges to their faith. Who better to help than those who themselves know the winter of the heart.

QUESTIONS FOR REFLECTION

1. Have you had troughs and peaks in your Christian journey? Have you also experienced them during other commitments and projects? How have you handled them?

2. Reflect on Lewis's notion of divine withdrawal. How could this understanding prove helpful when you are experiencing doubt and Absence?

7

Why Saint John of the Cross Can Give Us a Big Assist

Why the Dark Night of the Soul Is a Blessing

S aint John of the Cross (1542-91) provides the Christian tradition with the classic discussion of "the dark night of the soul." Indeed, we associate this very phrase with John of the Cross. If one is serious about this topic, this is where one turns. His writings are not as dark and somber as one might suspect, granting such a potentially bleak topic. They are, to the contrary, faith affirming and encouraging, even uplifting. So let's see what this great Christian mystic has to say. We can learn much from him.

John of the Cross believes, like Lewis, that this dark night is God's doing. So it is to be understood in that context. Moreover, it is designed for our spiritual improvement. It is something we are actually better off having. This is what he has to say:

It should be known, then, that God nurtures and caresses the soul, after it has been resolutely converted to His service, like a loving mother who warms her child with the heat of her bosom, nurses it with good milk and tender food, and carries and caresses it in her arms. But as the child grows older, the mother withholds her caresses and hides her tender love; she rubs bitter aloes on her sweet breast and sets the child down from her arms, letting it walk on its own feet so that it may put aside the habits of childhood and grow accustomed to greater and more important things.[1]

Thus the dark night of the soul becomes a stage, difficult and agonizing though it may sometimes be, through which one passes on the way to spiritual maturity, on the way "to greater and more important things." But how does this dark night benefit the soul?

The dark night of the soul is fundamentally a purging, John informs us, removing from us a range of faults and vices that often characterize those young in the faith (but not only them) with all their newfound zeal and earnestness. Importantly and first of all, it serves as a corrective to the beginner's tendency to spiritual pride. "These beginners," observed John, "feel so fervent and diligent in their spiritual exercises and undertakings that a certain kind of secret pride is generated in them . . . they condemn others who do not seem to have the kind of devotion they would like them to have."[2] I can recall, when

1. *John of the Cross: Selected Writings,* ed. Kieran Kavanaugh (New York: Paulist, 1987), p. 163.

2. *John of the Cross*, pp. 164-65.

just a couple of years into my own Christian journey, being critical of a minister whose devotional life consisted, as he informed us, of half an hour spent in prayer and Bible reading each morning. I judged this (silently to myself) to be insufficient and felt quite superior when comparing it with my then full hour each morning. I suppose I was in my own eyes twice as spiritual as he was! This particular episode was symptomatic of a more extensive malady — spiritual pride. But all sense of spiritual superiority is swept away, indeed crushed, with the dark night of the soul. Far from feeling spiritually superior and looking down on others, one seems to be hanging by a spiritual thread. One's spiritual condition is not sublime but wretched. One knows oneself to be a spiritual beggar, crying out to God, not a person standing aloof in confident judgment of others. If anything creates spiritual humility, it is the dark night of the soul.

Significantly, spiritual humility is not an isolated virtue. It bears good fruit in other areas of our life. It enables one to relate to others more graciously and to love them more sincerely than was possible before. Again, John speaks to us: "From this humility stems love of neighbor, for they will esteem them and not judge them as they did before when they were aware that they enjoyed an intense fervor while others did not."[3] Spiritual pride with its judgmental attitude toward others breeds contempt and inhibits love. It precludes a warm embrace of the other,

3. *John of the Cross*, p. 192.

which is essential if fellow pilgrims are to work together successfully for spiritual understanding, mutual support, and growth. I hesitate to conclude that spiritual pride is the inevitable condition of the new Christian, that, in other words, what was true of me is true of everyone in that newborn state. I suspect, however, that it is not rare and may be a condition especially prominent among the more spiritually earnest of our number. Certainly John thought so. And spiritual pride is not a vice unknown among veterans of the faith. However all this may be, the dark night of the soul is an effective antidote to spiritual pride. Of that there can be no doubt. This in turn removes one serious obstacle to a genuine love of neighbor.

John of the Cross sees yet another benefit, namely, a more respectful attitude toward God. Individuals who go through the dark night of the soul "commune with God more respectfully and courteously, the way one should always converse with the Most High. In the prosperity of their satisfaction and consolation as beginners, they did not act thus, for that satisfying delight made them somewhat more daring with God than was proper, and more discourteous and inconsiderate."[4] It is very easy, especially in evangelical circles, to be a bit too casual and comfortable in the presence of God. This may be a product of a certain excess in seeking to create an environment that generates and nourishes a personal and intimate relationship with God. To facilitate this close

4. *John of the Cross*, p. 190.

relationship, we may be tempted to downsize God. A small God is easier to relate to than a big God. This "friend we have in Jesus" becomes a buddy or pal. Consequently we show no more reserve and respect for God than we would show for a close personal friend with whom we feel free to joke, kid, and slap on the back. "Lord" becomes our hip pocket word for God, rather than a term of deep reverence and respect. "Our Lord is present!" — with this announcement there should be joy and excitement but also a strong inclination to sink to our knees. The danger is not merely that we show an improper respect for One who deserves infinitely more than we offer, but that we thereby distort our very understanding of God, who is now reduced to something less than God. Consequently, worship may miss its mark, being directed at something other than God. To be sure, this is not the only danger that the church faces. For we can also characterize God in ways that render him so remote and distant that personal connection is not possible. The church at large struggles on both scores. Nevertheless, it is the former danger that many of us face and for which the dark night of the soul may be our cure. But how does it do this, making us more respectful of God's majesty? Here we offer our own suggestions.

With the dark night of the soul spiritual matters become desperately serious. We no longer skip or sashay confidently into God's presence. A spiritual style characterized by froth and frivolity can find no home here. And our new status as desperate doubters possessed of a dryness of spirit, only underscores the vast disparity between what we are and the "majesty and grandeur" of the God we seek. We are now less inclined for purposes of ease of connection to reduce God to a mere replica of ourselves, the woe-begotten creatures we now see ourselves to be. As strange as it may seem, it is with God's apparent absence that God becomes bigger in our eyes.

Further, the dark night of the soul calls us to move beyond a self-serving and self-centered piety. This vice involves harnessing God's power, invoked principally through prayer, to enable one to flourish by standards provided not by the gospel but by the dominant culture to which one belongs. In our twenty-first-century United States this will often mean flourishing by the materialistic goals and consumerism that prevail in our society. Am I a success or am I a failure? It all depends on the things I have accumulated — homes, cars, clothes, bank accounts, promotions, prestige, etc. On such a compromised vision, God wants for us and will help us obtain just what our culture says we should want. All very convenient, of course. Here I am embedded in my culture energetically competing for all the "good" things it has to offer, a good life framed very much in materialistic terms, and I have one advantage over my fellow competitors: I am able to harness divine power to assist me in this life of accumulation. I have a "leg up" on my competition.

There is a threefold problem with this. First, the gospel that is to be at the center of our life has lost its independence over against the prevailing culture, to approve or disapprove what it offers. Second, God becomes our servant, much like the genie released from the bottle who is there to grant our wishes (at least three but hopefully many more). Third, we come to value God for what he can do for us and not for himself. We come to love the gifts more than the Giver. And when the gifts stop coming, we may be tempted to turn our backs on God and simply drift away. It is ourselves, it turns out, that we really love, and God has only instrumental value, important only for what he can do for us.

With the dark night of the soul the genie is no longer there to grant our every wish. God is no longer at our beck and call. By withdrawing, God communicates that he is not the servant of the person of faith, but it is the person of faith who is the servant. Moreover, it is God's kingdom and his will that are to be furthered by our efforts, energies, and prayers. At times this may place us at serious odds with the values of our culture and will call for sacrifices as defined by those values, perhaps forgoing financial advantage for ourselves or accolades from our community. The dark night of the soul, therefore, becomes an occasion for those of us whose piety has been self-centered and self-serving, to offer ourselves anew to God in a way that clarifies who commands and who follows, and for what ends.

We can perhaps add a further benefit to those John of the Cross has suggested: a new awakening of our love for God. With the presence of existential doubt we are, of course, painfully struggling with the absence of God. This divine absence, in many ways, is similar to the experience one has at the death of a parent, spouse, or very close friend. Too often — possibly more often than not — we come to appreciate all that such deceased persons have meant to us and all the good embodied in their lives only after they have been taken from us. We may hold them more dear and their memories more precious after their deaths than before. We see the extent of our loss and cannot help but reflect on the marvelous gift of their presence in our lives, a gift we no longer have. So it is with serious existential doubt. We greatly miss God's warm presence. Indeed, we agonize over God's absence. In essence, we mourn. Yet in new ways we begin to discover how much God all along has meant to us at the deepest levels of our being. Our deep feelings of love and loyalty are awakened from a kind of dormant slumber. This is by no means a uniquely religious phenomenon.

I can recall my first visit to the American cemetery at Omaha Beach in Normandy. There I had a deep emotional experience, one I had not anticipated having. It took me completely by surprise. I was there with students and had prepared them (with knowledge gained exclusively from my reading) for what we were about to see. But when I came into the cemetery and saw for the first time that sea of white crosses — so many crosses, row after row — each representing a life that had been given fighting the Nazi tyranny, many of those soldiers the same age as my students, I was overwhelmed with emotion. I looked at the American flag flying in the breeze and all those crosses, and I realized, as I never had before, for better or worse, how deeply American I was. These were deep feelings expressive of a profound love of country that had been there all along but were now powerfully coming to the surface. This simply was an occasion that triggered those feelings of love and loyalty. In a similar way our sense of God's absence may serve to bring to the surface how much our faith in God has meant to us and how much, even to our surprise, God is loved by us. This God who perplexes us and whose absence disturbs us is, wonder of wonders, deeply loved by us. This is a joyful discovery to make, and can help us grow yet further in our love for God. For we do love God, and we can build on that love. Fortunately, unlike the dead parent, spouse, or friend whose life cannot be restored to us short of eternity, with God we can have that restoration, accompanied by a new and deepened awareness of God as the One we are drawn to love with all our being.

In reflecting on these benefits associated with the dark night of the soul, one may wonder: Will any of this actually be of help to the person who is in the very midst of these spiritually troubling times? I cannot say for sure, and I cannot speak from personal experience because I had no such insights available to me when I experienced the darkest of those nights. I simply stumbled through. But to embrace those insights in the midst of the darkness, to see this as God's doing, is itself a movement away from that darkness and into the light. It is to recognize that we are in God's hands even in the darkness, even in the doubt. But equally important, the vision that Saint John of the Cross offers us may be of great value (as it has been for me) as we later look back on that dark night (or nights), even years later, seeing those spiritual benefits as gifts from God. We are then in a position to claim those benefits for ourselves, seeking to consolidate them by the grace of God in our lives: spiritual humility, reverencing God in his majesty and grandeur, abandoning a self-serving and self-centered piety, and coming to realize the depth of our love for God. Should there be such benefits, then one can only thank God for those dark nights. Now more than ever, "We know that God causes all things to work together for good to those who love God, to those who are called according to His purpose" (Rom. 8:28 NASB).

QUESTIONS FOR REFLECTION

1. John of the Cross views the dark night of the soul as a kind of purging that benefits the person of faith. What other benefits does John suggest? Can you think of additional benefits?

2. Do these benefits come automatically to us or must they be consciously appropriated in an act of Christian faith? Have you experienced such benefits, or are they still there waiting to be appropriated?

8

Why Mother Teresa's Dark Night of the Soul Has Much to Teach Us

If asked to name a person in our own day who most ex-
emplifies sacrificial love as a follower of Jesus Christ, I
suppose most of us would name Mother Teresa, founder
of the Missionaries of Charity, who gained worldwide
fame for her work in the slums of Calcutta among "the
poorest of the poor," the sick, the dying, the beggars, the
street children. Certainly one would be hard pressed to
think of a better choice. On the other hand, if asked who
wrote the following words, one of the last persons who
would come to mind, prior, that is, to the publication of
her letters, is Mother Teresa. Yet these are her words:

> since 49 or 50 this terrible sense of loss — this untold
> darkness — this loneliness — this continual longing for
> God — which gives me that pain deep down in my
> heart. — Darkness is such that I really do not see — nei-
> ther with my mind nor with my reason. — This place of
> God in my soul is blank. — There is no God in me. —
> When the pain of longing is so great — I just long & long

for God — and then it is that I feel — He does not want me — He is not here. — Heaven — souls — why these are just words — which mean nothing to me. — My very life seems so contradictory. I help souls — to go where? — Why all this? Where is the soul in my very being? God does not want me, — Sometimes — I just hear my own heart cry out — "My God" and nothing else comes. — The torture and pain I can't explain.[1]

For nineteen years Mother Teresa had been a Loreto nun in India involved in a teaching ministry. Then came her call to found what was to be called the Missionaries of Charity. She was confident that Jesus was speaking to her, calling her to start this new ministry, and confident that once begun it would prosper by God's blessing. She was to be, along with the sisters who were to labor with her, a carrier of God's love into the slums of Calcutta. Jesus' voice, she tells us, was pleading with her, "Come, come carry me into the holes of the poor. Come, be My light."[2] At this time in Mother Teresa's life there was no absent God, no silent Jesus, but a Jesus who was speaking to her and with whom she had a sacred dialogue. Confident of this call but obedient always to her superiors in the church, she sought their permission to do what the voice of Jesus was telling her to do. Impatient with what she

1. *Mother Teresa: Come Be My Light; The Private Writings of the "Saint of Calcutta,"* edited with commentary by Brian Kolodiejchuk, M.C. (New York: Doubleday, 2007), p. 210.

2. *Mother Teresa,* p. 44.

perceived to be the slow pace of gaining official approval, she pestered and pleaded with her superiors to speed up the process and grant her this permission. Finally that permission came and the new order was founded. She was joined by some former students she had taught as a Loreto nun. Then, after training and preparation, the work began. This was no limousine charity. Far from it. The sisters, in their Indian-like garb, were to share in the poverty of the poor, living in the slums with them. This was a very special and loving ministry that garnered worldwide attention.

It was shortly after the inception of the Missionaries of Charity that darkness descended and her spiritual struggles began in earnest: the darkness, the loneliness, the hungering for the God who was not there. She simply lacked the joy and consolation that come from God's felt presence. Deep down she found nothing but darkness and emptiness. The pain was almost unbearable as she felt "abandoned," "unwanted" by the One she loved with every fiber of her being. It was her intense love for God that made his absence so painful. Had there been no such love there would have been no such pain. For here the measure of one's love is the measure of one's pain. In Mother Teresa's case the love was great, and therefore so was the pain. We in similar circumstances may not have such distress, possibly because our love for God does not match hers.

All her struggles were shared with her spiritual advisers but kept hidden from the public, even from those sisters who labored by her side. When this was finally revealed with the publication of her letters, reactions were varied. Some felt, wrongly, that this somehow diminished the greatness of Mother Teresa. Others with very little religious understanding accused her of a kind of hypocrisy, pretending to be what she was not, a confident believer in the God of Jesus Christ. That latter charge is simply confused. For it was the sense of God's absence in her life that was disturbing to her, agonizingly so, not God's nonexistence. It was the absent God and not the nonexistent God who was at the heart of her struggles. Thus she speaks of her "longing for the Absent One."[3] She painfully writes, "there is such a deep loneliness in my heart that I cannot express it. . . . How long will Our Lord stay away?"[4] She was hungering for a strong sense of God's presence, the kind of presence she had known when she heard Jesus' voice calling her to found an order radically devoted to the poorest of the poor. Now that voice was silent and remained silent. Only when she asked for proof that God was pleased with the Missionaries of Charity did the darkness lift, and then for only a month. After that month she was plunged once more into darkness. "Our Lord," Mother Teresa wrote, "thought it better for me to be in the tunnel — so He is gone again — leaving me alone. — I am grateful for Him for the month of love He gave me."[5]

3. *Mother Teresa*, p. 165.
4. *Mother Teresa*, p. 158.
5. *Mother Teresa*, p. 177.

One is here reminded of C. S. Lewis's words (via the diabolical Screwtape): "some of His special favourites have gone through longer and deeper troughs than anyone else."[6] Mother Teresa would in her humility reject any suggestion that she was one of God's favorites. But we, who look in amazement at her sacrificial love for the poor manifested throughout her lifetime, would beg to differ. To be sure, God loves all of us with an infinite and everlasting love, but it would seem that those who hold nothing back from God, who love God so intensely and have such compassion for the poor, as Mother Teresa did, must have a special place in God's heart. If anyone qualifies as one of God's favorites, surely it is Mother Teresa. Certainly her life bears witness to the fact that some of those who have served God most faithfully and have been most effectively used by God have suffered the longest and the darkest of those nights. So as we struggle with our dark nights or look back upon them, we recognize that we are not alone in this regard, indeed that some of "God's favorites" have undergone longer and darker nights than we have had to endure. Although we can learn much from Mother Teresa's experience of darkness and her response to it, we do need to keep in mind that her situation is not altogether typical, being of such an extended length. As one of her advisers, commenting on her spiritual condition, observed, "it was simply the dark night of the soul which all masters of spiri-

6. C. S. Lewis, *The Screwtape Letters* (New York: Macmillan, 1957), p. 45.

tual life know — though I have never found it so deeply, and for so many years as in her."[7]

During her extended dark night Mother Teresa remained steadfastly faithful to her call, obedient to the work she was confident God had for her. "All these years I have only wanted one thing — to know and do the will of God. And now even in this hard and deep darkness — I keep on wanting only that. The rest he has taken all — and I think, He has destroyed everything in me — the only thing that keeps me on the surface — is obedience."[8] These certainly were hard times for Mother Teresa, and yet, as she firmly believed, all this — the loneliness, the sense of abandonment — was God's doing. Her response was simply to be a faithful servant of her absent Lord. Relevant to such an impressive fidelity are some other words from the diabolical Screwtape: "Our case is never more in danger than when a human, no longer desiring, but still intending to do our Enemy's will, looks round upon a universe from which every trace of Him seems to have vanished, and asks why he has been forsaken, and still obeys."[9] Mother Teresa also wondered why she had been forsaken, and possessed no strong and consoling sense of God's presence in her life, yet she remained faithfully obedient, year after year. Here is a dogged fidelity that can inspire us in our own struggles, though ours may not

7. *Mother Teresa*, p. 214.
8. *Mother Teresa*, p. 191.
9. Lewis, *The Screwtape Letters*, p. 47.

be so intense nor so lengthy, yet may be deeply challenging all the same. If ever something beautiful was offered to God, it was Mother Teresa's obedience amidst such darkness. And we too can offer something beautiful to God — faithfulness during our dark times.

Clearly Mother Teresa believed that the darkness to which she had been mysteriously consigned was God's doing and was to be so understood. Because it was God's doing, this darkness provided no reason to doubt the reality of God but only provided an occasion, extended though it was, to trust God and be obedient. When we, like Mother Teresa, experience no strong sense of God's presence in our lives, we may, unlike Mother Teresa, succumb to a kind of skepticism, doubting the very reality of God. Whereas it may be true (though in need of qualification) that "a person with an experience is never at the mercy of a person with an argument," nevertheless when that experience fades, one can become vulnerable to those skeptical considerations. At this dark juncture in our journey of faith, we are confronted with at least two possible interpretations, two different construals of what is happening to us: *a skeptical interpretation:* there is no God and for that reason there is no experience of God, and *a faith interpretation:* this is God's doing and he has his reasons. It was the latter interpretation that Mother Teresa unhesitatingly embraced, and it is this interpretation that we are invited to embrace should we experience these dark periods in our own lives. Why should we accept the faith interpretation?

George MacDonald commented that when a person is experiencing spiritual darkness and "can no longer *feel* the truth, he is able to know that he lives because he knows, having once understood the word that God is truth. He believes in the God of former vision, lives by that word therefore, when all is dark and there is no vision."[10] And so it was for Mother Teresa, who could look back upon times of close union and intimacy with her Lord, in essence able to believe "in the God of former vision." She had after all conversed with Jesus, who directed her to start this special ministry for the poorest of the poor. She did not doubt that the work of the Missionaries of Charity was God's work.[11] And this confidence remained throughout all the painful darkness. At times we too may have to live by our belief in the God of former vision, as we currently experience the Absence but remember the Presence and are true to it.

If God was responsible for the darkness that Mother Teresa experienced, as she resolutely believed, then the question naturally arises: Why? It may all be God's doing — that sense of Absence and for such a long time — but why? What is the point? What sense can be made of it? Clearly this is not a case of the darkness serving as a kind of purging or purification, as Saint John of the Cross advances, which is especially relevant for spiritual begin-

10. *George MacDonald: An Anthology,* ed. C. S. Lewis (New York: Macmillan, 1947), p. 13.
11. *Mother Teresa,* p. 187.

ners. We do not reject this interpretation because Mother Teresa had reached a state of sinless perfection, being free from all spiritual defects. No one reaches that state in this life. Indeed, as Father Kolodiejchuk comments, her letters reveal that the darkness with its pain and suffering "rendered her more kind hearted."[12] So even Mother Teresa gained spiritual benefits from the darkness. Nevertheless, the depth and length of the darkness and the sense of Absence in one so devoted to God and the poor do require a theological explanation. Though confident this was God's doing, she cried out for some explanation. And like the rest of us, she needed a theological interpretation of what was happening to her. She needed an answer to the question: Why was God doing this? When that answer finally came with the help of her spiritual adviser, the Jesuit theologian Father Joseph Neuner, she came "to love the darkness." But what was this understanding that gave rise to such a strange love, a love of the very darkness that caused such pain and gave rise to an agonizingly unrequited longing for God? How could one who so loved God, as Mother Teresa did, come to love such darkness?

Mother Teresa came to understand the "terrible darkness" that she experienced as part of her call to serve the needy and the forsaken, those apparently abandoned even by God. As Brian Kolodiejchuk, in his commentary on her letters, observed, "Her darkness was an identification with those she served. She was drawn mystically into

12. *Mother Teresa,* p. 166.

the deep pain they experienced as a result of feeling unwanted and rejected, and, above all, by living without faith in God."[13] It was also an identification with the death and passion of Jesus, who, crying out, "My God, my God, why have you forsaken me?" gave himself for the lost, the very lost that Mother Teresa was called to serve. With her darkness, then, Mother Teresa was mystically united both with her Lord and with the lost to whom she came to bring the light of God's love. This, then, was the spiritual side of her work and part therefore of her very call to serve the poorest of the poor, to serve them and be one with them in their abandonment.

Writing to Father Neuner, and thanking him for helping her to see this, Mother Teresa said, "For the first time in 11 years — I have come to love the darkness — For I believe now that it is a part, a very, very small part of Jesus' darkness and pain on earth. . . . Today really I felt a deep joy. . . . More than ever I surrender myself to Him. — Yes — more than ever I will be at his disposal."[14] Written in 1961, these words represented her vision of the darkness and its role in her life that was to inspire and console her to the end of her days. No doubt hers is a very special calling, not one extended to many, a calling in which the dark night of the soul is an integral part of the very ministry to which she has been appointed by God. Though special as it was, Mother Teresa's experience still inspires and in-

13. *Mother Teresa,* p. 216.
14. *Mother Teresa,* p. 214.

structs. There was her faithfulness during dark times when she was bereft of any theological understanding of what was happening to her; there was a faith that wondered what God was doing but not whether there was a God who was doing it; there was a deep, intense love of God that increased the pain of the darkness but also kept her ready to sacrifice all in the service of her God. Finally, was God present in her life? Yes, of course he was. As Father Neuner commented, "The sure sign of God's hidden presence in this darkness is the thirst for God, the craving for at least a ray of His light. No one can long for God unless God is present in his/her heart."[15] And few have longed for and loved God like Mother Teresa.

<hr>

QUESTIONS FOR REFLECTION

1. Do you think less of Mother Teresa for having experienced extended periods when she felt no sense of God's presence? Should you?

2. Mother Teresa found great consolation — indeed, she came to love the darkness — upon embracing the theological interpretation that Father Neuner, her spiritual adviser, suggested to her. Why is it important to have a

15. *Mother Teresa*, p. 214.

satisfactory theological understanding of those dark times during our journey of faith?

3. Can C. S. Lewis or John of the Cross play a role for us similar to the one Father Neuner played for Mother Teresa? Can you think of other theological interpretations of those dark times of faith that might also prove helpful?

9

*Why Hope Can Be the Basis
for Faith during Hard Times*

*Why Hope Rather Than Doubt
Should Guide Our Lives*

Why God Loves Hopers

When individuals are undergoing prolonged doubt about God's reality and the truth of the Christian message, they may come to the point where belief seems to have vanished. It is not that they disbelieve, embracing the opposite conviction that there is no God and the Christian faith is false. It is rather that belief, the positive conviction that it is true, is missing. It once was strongly present, but it is no longer. It is uncertainty, not outright disbelief, that possesses the citadels of their hearts and minds. Erroneously, they may think that the only basis for faith is belief. I must believe, they say to themselves. I must at least have the confidence that it is more likely than not that I am in possession of the truth. If I don't, all is lost. Faith is no longer possible, they fear. But to the contrary, all is not lost. Faith is still possible. For existential doubters who find themselves caught right in this middle ground between belief and disbelief, there is always hope, and hope can legitimately serve as a basis for continuing faith in the absence of a more confident belief. Just as faith in the sense of trust and commitment can be based on knowledge or on a belief short of knowledge, so also faith in that important sense can be based on hope. This would be faith in what one hopes to be true, and hope-based faith can tide one over during those dark times, however long and troublesome they may be. It can serve as a bridge, perhaps temporary, between one's initial confidence and the subsequent return of that confidence. So some of us may be knowers, others believers, and still others hopers, but all of us are people of faith, placing our faith (trust) in the God and Father of Jesus Christ and committing ourselves to building a life around that hope.

Importantly, it needs to be noted that the everyday and more familiar concept of hope appropriated and used in this chapter is not to be confused with the robust, confident, and very special vision of hope we associate with New Testament teachings. But this robust confidence and the biblical hope generated by it is simply not where doubters find themselves, uncertain as they are and wondering about it all. What they need is a weaker sense of hope, one capable of accommodating their uncertainty and serving as a temporary placeholder until hearts and minds once again reverberate with the confidence that is at the heart of New Testament hope. What is offered to meet this need is a notion of hope, as common as it may be, that has great value for our lives even apart from its use during those dark times in our spiritual journey. This sense of hope has a wider application than the biblical notion that is exclusively oriented toward the future and confidently anticipates what God will bring to pass (cf. Rom. 8:24-25). In contrast, the notion of hope we will employ can be directed to the past or the present as well as the future, and can helpfully serve as a basis for continued faith during extended times of doubt and uncertainty. Also, it will continue to have an important place in our lives even when we do find ourselves possessed by the "sure and certain hope" given expression in the biblical text. For there will always be important areas of life, apart from the religious, where matters are rightly acknowledged to be uncertain and where hope can and should be a controlling dynamic in our lives. What precisely is this notion of hope, and how can it provide a basis for faith during those times when knowing and believing are in short supply?[1]

To hope that something is the case, you must *want* it to be the case. Wanting or desiring is a necessary and significant component of hope. This is the first thing we should notice about it. It is in just this way that hoping differs from believing. I can, for instance, sensibly say I *believe*

1. In what follows I am very much indebted to James L. Muyskens, *The Sufficiency of Hope* (Philadelphia: Temple University Press, 1979).

Jones will win the race but I don't want him to win. In contrast, I can't sensibly say I *hope* Jones will win the race but I don't want him to. What you hope for must be what you want to be the case. If I hope Jones will win, then I want him to win. In contrast, believing that something is the case says nothing about what you want. In believing something to be true, you may or may not want it to be true, indeed you might be utterly indifferent. But hope is quite different. When you hope, you care. There is something at stake that matters to you. So when what I believe to be true turns out to be false, I'll be surprised, but when what I hope to be true turns out to be false, I'll be disappointed. This fact reflects the desire component of hope.

Because hoping involves wanting something to be true, our hopes tell us more about ourselves than our beliefs usually do. Few things reveal more about us than the hopes we have for ourselves, our family, our friends, our nation, and our world. We get a good fix on a person's character by finding out what that person hopes for. We can examine ourselves by taking a good look at our own hopes. If our Christian faith does anything for us, it should shape our hopes and give birth to new ones. Further, because hoping involves wanting or desiring, our hopes can be morally evaluated. What we desire to be true may be good or evil or just indifferent, and so consequently our hopes, which contain those desires, may be good or evil or indifferent. Our hopes, then, can be morally assessed in a way that our beliefs typically cannot be. Reflect on the difference between saying I *believe* the president will be assassinated and saying I *hope* the president will be assassinated. To the first statement an appropriate response would be: "Why do you believe that?" To the second it would be: "Shame on you! You shouldn't hope for any such thing."

We now see how hope differs from belief. It is the desire component that distinguishes hope from mere belief. Hope also differs from *wishing* in an important respect. Hoping is not simply wishful thinking. And this is important to note because skeptics often accuse religious believers of wishful thinking. But hoping is not wishing. The two are altogether different concepts: I can *wish* for what I believe to be impossible, but I cannot *hope* for what I believe to be impossible. I can, for example, wish that my father, for whom I have much affection and who died a number of years ago, were still alive. I cannot, however, *hope* that my father is still alive, which I know to be an impossibility. So to hope that something is true there must be some possibility (in the hoper's judgment) that it is true. As long as there is at least some realistic possibility (not a mere logical possibility), hope can find a foothold. So even when one hopes, there must be some reason to think that what one hopes for *might* be true, that the possibility has not been ruled out. Should it be ruled out in one's thinking, then one can only wish and no longer hope.

Hope is not, then, a substitute for thinking and reasoning. It still has to be successfully argued that what is hoped for is a realistic possibility. Certainly the hoper has fewer intellectual demands than does the believer or the

85

knower. Nevertheless, there are demands all the same. Possibilities can be sufficiently remote that hope can become foolish, bordering on wishful thinking. I can hope I'll win the California lottery, but this hope cannot be taken seriously, the chances of winning being too remote. But if I had a fifty-fifty chance of winning, or even a one-in-ten chance, my hope understandably could be rather robust. So what I hope for must be possible, but it can't be certain. In the hoper's eyes the matter must be uncertain. I can't, for example, hope I'm a male or that I'm a U.S. citizen, both of which I confidently know to be true. Certainty and hope are incompatible. In summary, then, hope operates in the domain of the uncertain but possible. And this is just where doubters find themselves. So let's see how hope can be of help.

The God one sees in Jesus and finds portrayed in the larger biblical witness is a God of power, wisdom, and love. Such a God is eminently worthy of our complete trust — if God exists, that is. But does he? This is just what doubters wonder, torn, at least for the present, between belief and unbelief. But for doubters there is always hope, and that hope can be the basis of trust and commitment — trust that they have been created for good purposes, that God through Christ extends to them (and to all) a loving and forgiving embrace, that God calls them to a life of servant love, that death will not ultimately defeat God's good purposes for them, that God will insure that justice, love, and beauty will ultimately triumph over injustice, hatred, and ugliness. This is what they desire to be true, and their desires are honorable and good. This is where they put their trust, and trust always involves risk. For hopers, as well as for believers, trust takes the form of putting their energies, efforts, resources, and prayers (yes, hopers pray too) in the service of the purposes they discern God has for them and for all people. They are willing to sacrifice. They extend thanks, praise, and worship to this One whose reality is the object of their hope. They do not abandon their Christian commitment. They continue to trust, to commit; that is, to have faith.

To be sure, in their present state they acknowledge that they could be wrong, but what they hope for is nevertheless a real possibility, not a pipe dream, and what a possibility it is! Yes, one could be wrong; but one could also be right. This is a possibility too great to pass up, to drift away from, to allow doubts rather than hopes to shape one's life. After all, people have bravely fought wars they were not certain they could win, persisted in seeking cures for diseases in the face of repeated failures, pursued the dream of getting a novel published despite a stack of rejection slips, relentlessly searched the earth for mineral wealth that just might be there, and in a myriad of ways pursued hoped-for possibilities. But theirs, they judge, is the greatest of possibilities, and so they remain faithful. How, they ask, could they do otherwise?

Our Christian hopers are of the conviction that building their life around the God and Father of Jesus Christ is their best chance (they do not presume to speak for all others) to connect with, maintain, and nourish a relationship with *the Creator of the universe and the source of all meaning.* So they remain faithful and commit wholeheartedly. Even if they could be wrong, even if in their present thinking it is but a fifty-fifty proposition, nevertheless the significance of its being true is so great that it warrants faithfulness and commitment. Indeed, what could be more significant? When people, unlike our hoper, back away from such commitment, it's not simply because of the uncertainty — "I just don't know" — but rather it's because — and let's be honest — they don't place a high value on the possibility of being connected to God — "I don't care that much." The mere possibility of God and all that this possibility entails is not for them sufficiently motivating. So it's not the uncertainty that finally deters them from a life of faith but rather the lower value they place on what for hopers is not merely a possibility but a staggering and compelling possibility.

Perhaps there is a special place in God's heart for hopers who maintain their faith amidst some agony of soul, who want God to exist and who seek to live their lives in accord with the perceived will of this God who is the object of their hope. Possibly we place too much emphasis on mere belief. What my wife wants from me is not merely that I believe that she exists. That is to offer her too little. What she wants from me is to *want* her to exist, to rejoice in her existence, to be thankful for her existence. Similarly, by itself the belief that God exists amounts to very little, a fact that has received scriptural recognition: "Even the demons believe — and shudder"

(James 2:19 RSV). A hoper, in contrast, shudders at the thought that God does not exist.

I may, of course, want God to exist because of the benefits I believe I can receive from God. To find myself in a world bereft of God may be terrifying, and my hope that God exists may be rooted in a desire for a kind of comfort, security, and meaning that only God can bring. There is nothing wrong with this. This is something we all understandably want. This may not, however, exhaust all the desires that the hoper has in hoping. The hoper may want God to exist simply because of who God is. How much poorer reality would be if there is not this One in whom all perfections inhere: perfect love, power, knowledge, and beauty. All this and more in one majestic Being, who will secure his good purposes for the world he has created. Wanting this Being to exist gets close — very close — to what is meant by love of God. And it makes sense to think that our relationship with God will ultimately be determined by our wanting God to exist, not simply by believing that God exists. In the end, it is likely that our salvation is played out in the context of our deepest desires and yearnings, what we, in essence, hope for. Belief that God exists is a blessing when coupled with a yearning for God, but if we had to choose between belief and yearning, and could have one but not the other, here there is no doubt, we choose yearning. All those who want God to exist, no matter what travails of soul they experience, will in the end come to believe, indeed to know. Such, at least, is our hope.

QUESTIONS FOR REFLECTION

1. Have you had times in your Christian journey when you would have characterized yourself as a knower? a believer (short of knowing)? a hoper? As you moved in or toward the hoper category, did you tend to view yourself as somehow spiritually subpar? Or as you viewed others in that category, did you tend to view them as spiritually deficient?

2. In continuing to exercise faith based on hope, one has placed a high value on the possibility of being connected to God. In what way is turning to or turning away from God in such circumstances primarily a value judgment and not, as we often think, a question of evidence?

10

*Why the Christian Community
Is the Best Place to Doubt*

*Why Going to Church Matters
Even When You Get Little out of It*

One of the best pieces of advice doubters can receive is to live out their doubts in the context of the Christian community. Here a decision is called for — the decision to struggle with doubt and a sense of Absence in the context of the Christian church, in fellowship with other Christians. After all, you are going to do this either within the church or outside the church. Decide to do it within the church. It is not as if a fair-minded person should or even could do this in some completely neutral context. There is, it so happens, no such neutral context. Even those fully connected to the church — except for monks — will still live the bulk of their lives in the secular environment that our culture provides. Fair-mindedness does not require that in critically and honestly reflecting on one's religious commitment one disengage from the church and inhabit an exclusively secularized world, a world minus God and devoid of any expression of the Christian faith. That is far from creating an even playing field. Moreover, how can one withdraw from the very thing that one is putting to the test: the church's affirmations and the way of life it offers?

Of course, sometimes the church, the local congregation where one worships and fellowships, has become part of the problem. Indeed, some people turn away from the Christian faith because they mistakenly identify the Christian faith exclusively with a particular expression of that faith that they, rightly or wrongly, find objectionable. But the church at large contains a wide range of liturgical and musical styles, preaching styles, theological and political sympathies, etc. These are communities, though different in certain respects, where the gospel is honored and Christ is present. In connecting with a church that best serves your needs and where you can be at home with your struggles, remember that the perfect church does not exist. But neither does the perfect family, workplace, school, or political party. The church is no different in this regard. It too is made up of flawed, even if forgiven, human beings. And if you ever did find a church that you liked without qualification, a church that perfectly met all your needs and expectations, you would most likely be the only person in attendance — a church just for you! In fact, it would have to be designed with only you in mind, disregarding all the other good folks with their very different needs and expectations, who also require a church home. Always keep in mind that we live in an imperfect world and that churches are no exception. In working with people and organizations, including the church, we should have realistic expectations. So maintain a strong connection with a Christian fellowship, one that best meets your needs, even though not perfectly.

In deciding to struggle with our doubts and uncertainties within the context of the Christian community, we have decided to continue to participate in the Christian form of life on its own terms. This is crucial. It is a decision not to abandon the means whereby Christians believe God communicates and communes with us: prayer, Scripture, meditation, proclamation, worship. Ultimately what can be known about the Christian faith, its truth or falsity, its saving and transforming power, cannot be known from the outside by detached reflection, like anthropologists studying the religious beliefs and practices of some "primitive" tribe without immersing themselves in that alien way of life. It is within the Christian community and its form of life that the true nature of that faith is to be found and understood. Hence the importance of continued connection to the Christian community even when wondering at some level about what it all amounts to.

For the person going through a period of dryness or undergoing substantial doubt, church attendance may lose much of its relish. Sermons do not inspire; the music does not touch one's heart. Church attendance has become a chore rather than a joy. In those circumstances one may very well ask, "What's the point? I'm not getting anything out of it, so why should I even go to church?" But there *is* a point to it, and a very important point at that. For attending church, gathering with others for worship, is fundamentally an expression of loyalty and an act of deep respect. And this has value and significance apart from what we get out of it. Showing this respect for God is a central feature of the Christian life, and may take on special importance during the dark times in one's journey of faith, or when one is in a trough period, to invoke Lewis's law of undulation. Let me attempt to explain this with a personal story.

On one Sunday morning while traveling in Europe with a group of twenty-five students the decision was made to attend church together. The church we chose to visit turned out to be a small congregation, so small that our presence doubled the attendance. Quite naturally the service (Scripture, hymns, sermon) was conducted in the language of the country we were visiting, and none of us, it so happened, was fluent enough to fully comprehend what was being said, read, or sung. There were glimmerings of understanding, but they were minimal. When the service was concluded the regular worshipers gathered together, chatted with one another and talked with what I took to be a visiting minister. We, on the other hand, were completely ignored — not a greeting of any kind, not so much as a friendly nod or a smile, not even a glance was sent in our direction as they chatted away amongst themselves. There didn't seem to even be any curiosity about who we were and why we were worshiping with them. We felt invisible, and for all practical purposes we were. We stood around briefly and rather awkwardly, and then filed out of the church feeling a bit deflated. We had understood very little of what had gone on in the service, and on top of that our reception had been rather chilly. Certainly not much to write home about. As we gathered outside, I wondered what I could say that would put a helpful perspective on what had just transpired. Had this all been a complete waste of time? Would the time have been better spent back at the hotel in bed or having a leisurely breakfast? It would be tempting to think so. I wanted, however, to deny that that was the case. Quite the contrary, I wanted to affirm that what we had just done, despite all the negatives, was spiritually important. But how to communicate this?

Some words of Pascal, the seventeenth-century scientist, philosopher, and theologian, came to mind, and I shared them. "Respect means; put yourself out. That may look pointless, but it is quite right, because it amounts to saying: I should certainly put myself out if you needed it, because I do so when you do not; besides, respect serves to distinguish the great. If respect meant sitting in an armchair we should be showing everyone respect and then there would be no way of marking distinction, but we make the distinction quite clear by putting ourselves out."[1] Admittedly, I could quote from memory only the first five words of the quotation: "Re-

---

1. Blaise Pascal, *Pensées* (London: Penguin Books, 1966), #80.

spect means; put yourself out." Pascal is not talking about church attendance, but his remarks have a ready application to that custom. He is referring to customs that in our day are largely disappearing, for example, standing up when an older person, a woman, or a dignitary enters the room, or doffing one's hat on meeting such a person on the street (when men regularly wore hats). In Pascal's day a person would kneel or bow before a monarch to show appropriate respect, a custom that continues in some places to this day — think of the queen of England. These are all acts, to use Pascal's words, of "putting oneself out." And *that,* I pointed out to my students, was *exactly* what we had just done. We had put ourselves out, thereby affirming our loyalty and respect for our God. Pascal is not thinking of dramatic sacrificial acts but of small, seemingly inconsequential acts of paying respect that are scattered across the terrain of one's life: standing up, doffing one's hat, to which I have added, going to church. On that Sunday morning in Europe we had gotten out of bed, had eaten a hurried breakfast, had walked to the church and spent an hour there. We had put ourselves out. We had knelt before our King. And putting oneself out, thereby showing one's respect, is arguably the most significant part of church attendance. For where else can we show this respect? Where else can we go? How else shall we do it?

It is not only what we receive from the worship service by way of inspiration and instruction that renders it spiritually significant. To be sure, these benefits are not inconsequential, and we rightly want inspiration and helpful instruction, but their absence does not mean our presence at church has thereby become pointless. Far from it. For we have, after all, put ourselves out. We have paid our respects. We have given public expression to our loyalties. And "putting ourselves out" on that Sunday morning in Europe began when we got out of bed, dressed, and walked to that church. Worship in that sense did not begin when we entered the church doors and sat down in a pew. So it is for all Sunday mornings. Even when one is not struggling with one's faith, there can be periods — and we've all experienced them — when going to church seems to be nothing more than "going through the motions." And it is often put in just that way. But bear in mind that with those motions, as mechanical as they may sometimes feel, we are still "putting ourselves out," paying respect to One eminently worthy of that respect. So even going through the motions is a spiritually significant exercise. "Respect serves to distinguish the great," says Pascal, and by church attendance we seek to do just that.

The relevance of all this to those dark nights is this. Amidst our doubts we need to continue to affirm our loyalty and show our respect. And church is where we do this. On those Sunday mornings, week after week, month after month, we put ourselves out, thereby helping to prevent other attractions and other possibilities from usurping the place of the One who is to be our ultimate loyalty and our first love. To do otherwise is to decide in favor of those other possibilities. But no, even during the dark times we pay our respects and wait patiently for grace. We put ourselves in a place where God has been known to speak and where he had spoken to us in days gone by. One never knows when fire will strike and our hearts will be deeply moved by that sermon or that hymn or that prayer. So we pay our respects and wait patiently.

QUESTIONS FOR REFLECTION

1. Have you ever gone to church — even for a period of time — when it seemed like you were simply going through the motions? Did you therefore conclude that your churchgoing lacked any real spiritual significance? Have you ever challenged that negative conclusion?

2. Why is the decision by the doubter to continue to meet in worship with other Christians a crucial decision? Why is it part of a strategy of putting doubt in its place? Has it been part of your strategy?

11

Why Unanswered Prayer Can Be a Problem

*Why We Should Love God More Than We Love
What God Can Do for Us*

Why We Shouldn't Sell Prayer Short

Some of the most troubling times in our journey of
faith occur when in great need we cry out to God for
help but help does not come. Again and again we pray,
perhaps for someone we love dearly, perhaps to avert
some great tragedy, but we are met only with silence and
our prayers go unanswered. It has been said in response
to these challenging realities that God *always* answers
prayer. It's just that at times the answer is yes and our petition is granted, but at other times the answer is no and
for God's own good reasons our petition is denied. So
whether it's a yes or a no, there is always a divine response. But that no doesn't seem like an answer. Rather it
seems as if one has been speaking into a void. We wonder
whether the prayer goes unanswered because God in his
sovereign wisdom has decreed it so, *or* because there is

only the void, *or* because — heaven forbid! — God just doesn't care. And so, we wonder, how are we to interpret these mysterious silences that accompany our life of prayer?

One of the serious challenges to our Christian faith is the danger of loving what God can do for us — usually via the medium of petitionary prayer — more than God himself. And we certainly do love what God can do for us. Of that there can be no doubt. To be struck by a life-threatening illness and to pray and then to be healed. To be uncertain about a crucial decision, with so much depending on it, and to pray and then make a decision where things work out wonderfully. To have an obstacle in the way of a worthy personal or professional goal, and then to have God remove it for us. To have a financial need and to pray and then have that need fully met. How we love it! And who wouldn't? To have an infinite power at our disposal, smoothing our way through life, saving us from disaster, giving us the inside track to success. What could be better?

But right here is the danger: if we love what God can do for us more than we love God himself, then when God doesn't seem to be doing all those good things that we ask him to do, our faith may falter and be placed in serious jeopardy. For what we *really* love is no longer there. For after all, what is God good for if he doesn't ward off danger, cure illness, meet financial needs, solve personal problems, give clear direction in the midst of perplexity, and do all this with a fair degree of regularity? If this is what is *cen-*

tral to our faith in God, if this is the *magnet* that attracts us and holds us to things Christian, if this is what we *really* love, it will be only a matter of time before our faith is under siege. For what will happen when we find ourselves in the shoes of the prophet Habakkuk, exclaiming: "O LORD, how long shall I cry for help, / and thou wilt not hear" (Hab. 1:2 RSV)? Or what will happen when the words of the psalmist are on our lips: "O my God, I cry by day, but thou dost not answer; / and by night, but find no rest" (Ps. 22:2 RSV)? Or when the apostle Paul's experience becomes our experience — Paul, who three times prayed that the mysterious thorn in the flesh might be removed (and Paul, keep in mind, was a pretty tough customer), but it was not to be? Or when, in some small measure, we can identify with Jesus in the Garden of Gethsemane, who prayed, "My father, if it is possible, let this cup pass from me"? But it was not possible. All this is part of the Christian experience. Indeed, it is part of the biblical portrayal of faith's journey. None of us is exempt. There will be such times in all of our lives — difficult times, challenging times, maybe prolonged times — when in response to our cries for help the power of God is not unleashed for our benefit. As C. S. Lewis commented, every gravestone is a monument to unanswered prayer. These are times when our needs are great but the heavens are not responsive. And during these times it is imperative that we have a love for God that is greater than the love we have for what God can do for us.

But perhaps in these trying times, God is not totally silent; perhaps if we listen carefully, we can hear his voice: "Do you love me? Do you love me more than what I can do for you?" So the next time a prayer for something important seemingly goes unanswered, and the heavens seem so silent, we should listen carefully for that voice — "Do you love me? Do you love me more than you love what I can do for you?" And may we be able to respond: "Yes, Lord, we love you. Help us to love you more." Possibly one very important reason why our prayers are not always answered is that God wants us to come to love him more than we love his gifts. For at some point God must begin to wean us from a love for those gifts and to a greater love for himself. And when we do come to love the Lord our God with all our heart and with all our soul and with all our mind and with all our strength, we will have come to love God more than we love all that God can do for us — indeed much more. This thought was captured beautifully in a prayer by George Matheson: "Whether Thou comest in sunshine or in rain, I would take Thee into my heart joyfully. Thou art Thyself more than the sunshine; Thou art Thyself compensation for the rain. It is Thee and not Thy gifts that I crave." Therefore, we do well to nourish a love for God. In our heart and on our lips may it also be: "It is Thee and not Thy gifts that I crave." If that be so, unanswered prayer will be much less of a threat to faith's constancy.

It is also important to recognize that if God answered all our prayers, we, not God, would rule the universe. If the president of the United States did everything *I* asked him to do, he would cease to be president — he would be replaced by me. So also, if God answered all our prayers we would be deciding who wins wars and who loses, who lives and who dies, who is healed and who is not — *we* would govern the universe by our prayers and God would be abdicating his role as Sovereign Lord. But God is sovereign and we are not. And it is this Sovereign Lord whose eternal purposes are being worked out in and through this world of ours, a world made up of an incredibly complicated system of intertwining causes and effects. It is through this labyrinth that God is working his will, and it may be, at least in some cases, though unknown to us, that by answering a particular prayer, though legitimate and honorable in every respect, the pursuit of some of those divine purposes would be blocked. We may not know when this is the case, but we acknowledge that there may well be such instances and ours may be one of them.

And, of course, God cannot answer all our prayers because people sometimes pray for contradictory things. A farmer prays for rain and a homeowner in a nearby mudslide area prays that it won't rain. Warring adversaries pray for God to intervene on their behalf to secure victory for them. Moreover, there may be times when it's not in our interest to have our requests granted. On one occasion the mother of James and John asked Jesus if her sons might have places of special privilege in the kingdom of heaven, sitting on his right and left hand. Wouldn't that be wonderful! — or so she thought. Jesus replied, "You do not know what you are asking." What she did not know was that those places of honor were reserved for those who were to die a martyr's death, not a fate she would wish for her sons. And so with many of our prayers, we pray in ignorance, and we don't realize the consequences that will accompany our getting what we ask for. And the kindest thing God could do for us is simply not to grant our request. So we recognize that *for our sakes* not all our prayers should be answered.

But let's not sell God and prayer short. In one scene from Alfred Lord Tennyson's *The Idylls of the King,* King Arthur is taking leave of a friend and he says to him:

> If thou shouldst never see my face again,
> Pray for my soul. More things are wrought by prayer
> Than this world dreams of. Wherefore, let thy voice
> Rise like a fountain for me night and day.

Some answers to prayer are clear and unambiguous, at least to the person of faith. At other times it takes discernment to see that God *has* answered our prayer. Should discernment be lacking, the answer will go unrecognized. In this regard, God sometimes denies us the *details* of our prayer but nonetheless gives us the desire of our heart, which is an answer to prayer. Many centuries ago a young man was about to sail from North Africa for Italy. The young man was a pagan. His mother was a Christian who prayed all that night through in a nearby seaside chapel. She prayed that her son might not sail and thereby leave the orbit of her Christian influence. He was headed for Rome with all its many temptations. She felt that if he went to Italy all hope for his conversion would be lost. So she prayed all the night long. But even as she was on her knees praying that God would change the mind of her son, the ship was setting sail and her son was aboard and headed for Italy. But in Italy this man came under the profound influence of Ambrose, bishop of Milan, and he was converted from his paganism to the Christian faith. The name of the mother who had prayed so faithfully the night through in that seaside chapel was Monica. The name of her son was, of course, Augustine, arguably the most influential of all postapostolic Christians. So did God answer Monica's prayer? The details of her prayer were denied but the desire of her heart was granted, and surely that is an answer to prayer. God did what Monica wanted but did it his way, not hers.

Other prayers God answers by changing our desires. And one of the real possibilities in prayer is that God will redirect our desires. We go into prayer asking for one thing, and we come out desiring something else — possibly what we already have. Or we become reconciled to our current circumstances as being God's will, and we seek and receive strength to confront the challenge or bear the burden. Sometimes God answers our prayer in the way we asked but much later, possibly years later — and time has dulled our memory so that we fail to recognize it as an answer to our prayer. One thinks of prayers offered for the spiritual welfare of friends or family members. Sometimes we may not live to see the return of the prodigal son or daughter, but eventually the prodigal returns and our prayer is answered. So Tennyson may be right: "More things are wrought by prayer than this world dreams of."

But we make a mistake if we think of prayer as chiefly asking God for favors. In prayer we seek God's forgiveness, we express gratitude for the many good things in our life, we praise God for who he is, we share our hopes and dreams, and so forth. Even when prayer is going swimmingly — petitions are being granted one after another — asking God for things nevertheless remains but a small part of a normal and healthy prayer life. After all, prayer should be centered around God, not around ourselves. And when we are experiencing a sense of Absence, we should not stop praying. We should continue to confess our sin and to make our requests, but above all we should thank God for the good things he has brought into our lives, and praise God for who and what he is. During the dark times, amidst our doubt and confusion, we should focus on what we are thankful for and give expression to this in prayer. And we should do this daily. For what links the receiver of a gift (that's you and me) to the giver of the gift (that's God, the giver of every good and perfect gift) is gratitude. Without gratitude the link is broken. But gratitude requires practice, like improving a golf swing or acquiring a new language. We have to work at it. Each day thank God for some good thing in your life. It can be something big or small, but do it regularly. Also, each day praise God for a particular attribute of his — his love, his holiness, his majesty, etc. Pray to the silence if that is your condition, but keep praying, praising, and expressing gratitude. And see if Absence doesn't become Presence.

Finally, it is crucial to recognize that to do business with God in prayer, we are not required to come with a faith free of doubt and uncertainty. The only requirement is that we come. Doubts do not cut one off from God. Reflect on the Gospel account of the father who comes to Jesus with his epileptic son for healing (Mark 9:14-29). The father had first approached the disciples of Jesus, but they were unable to help. So, in his continuing desperation, he turns to Jesus (who had just come down from the Mount of Transfiguration). The man approaches Jesus and says: "Teacher, I brought my son to you, for he is possessed by a spirit, and wherever it seizes him, it dashes him down; and he foams and grinds his teeth and becomes rigid." The father also informs Jesus that the son had been like this since early childhood. So the son and the father had both suffered much over the years: the son because of his condition and the father because of his love for his son. The man therefore implores Jesus: "If you can do anything, have pity on us and help us." One can feel, many centuries later, as one reads these words, the pain in this man's plea. Jesus replies that it is not a matter of what he can do, but of what the man can do. For "all things are possible to him who believes." The man quickly monitors the status of his own heart and mind, which he knows is a mixture of doubt and uncertainty, on the one hand, and belief and hope, on the other. But this is too important an occasion to play games — to pretend to be something that one is not. For if this Jesus can heal his son, he can also discern the man's heart. So in utter honesty the father cries out: "I believe; help my unbelief." And in response the son is healed. The epilepsy, the demonic presence, is banished, gone forever. The man's belief was less than perfect, but it was sufficient, and so will be our belief as well. The father's words can be our words as we gather in worship, kneel in prayer, and open the pages of Scripture. "Lord, I believe; help my unbelief." That is enough.

—∞∞—

QUESTIONS FOR REFLECTION

1. Has prayer been a source of encouragement or discouragement or possibly both at different times in your journey of faith?

2. What can we do to nurture a love for God so that Matheson's words ("It is Thee and not Thy gifts that I crave") can be truthfully on our lips as well?

3. "Unanswered prayer" calls for an interpretation. Some interpretations may lead us away from God, others closer to God. How so? Can you speak to this from your own experience?

12

Why It's Important to Come to Terms with the Fact That Many People Reject What You Believe

Why Disagreement Shouldn't Preclude Strong Commitment

Many Christians find it very unsettling and doubt inducing to discover that many people reject the very beliefs they hold as Christians. Of course, at a theoretical level they have known this all along. After all, their working vocabulary includes the words "atheist," "agnostic," "secular humanist," "Hindu," "Buddhist," "Muslim," and "Jew." This is an acknowledgment that the world is filled with people who embrace alternative spiritual and secular visions, and therefore disagree with them. But a theoretical recognition of this fact is one thing and an actual encounter with these differences in the flesh is something else again, as when one enters a university community for the first time or one becomes acquainted with people of different religious persuasions. What should our response be to this widespread disagreement?

In the seventeenth century Pascal observed that the

fact of religious disagreement is often put forward as a reason for making no commitment at all. "Those who do not love truth," he wrote, "excuse themselves on the grounds that it is disputed and that very many people deny it."[1] Not much has changed since then. I was once invited to have breakfast with the father of one of my students. The student had arranged this in hopes that I might be able to address some of the skeptical concerns that her father had about the Christian faith. In talking with him, I discovered that he was quite active in state politics on behalf of one of the major political parties. It was his consuming passion. As our discussion moved in the direction of religion and Christianity, prompted by his daughter, he offered as a reason for shying away from any religious commitment the fact that there is so much disagreement, so many different religions. And even within religious traditions there is much disagreement and fragmentation. "What is a man to believe?" he asked. What was interesting about his response was his apparent inconsistency. Whereas religious disagreement was offered as a reason to not make a religious commitment, political disagreement did not prevent him from making serious political commitments (nor should it have). Certainly when one looks at the American political landscape, let alone the world at large, one sees as much disagreement and as many competing perspectives as one finds in the religious realm, but my student's father was not thereby

---

1. Blaise Pascal, *Pensées* (London: Penguin Books, 1966), #176.

deterred from making a political commitment and becoming an enthusiastic advocate at that.

Moreover, when one moves from issues of politics to issues of morality and ethics, one is confronted with the same challenge — so many differing perspectives, accompanied by interminable and heated debate. But we do not shy away from moral commitments on the grounds that "it is disputed." Indeed, it is the very fact of disagreement that fuels our passion and prompts us to become advocates. If everyone agreed with us, there would be neither the passion nor the need for advocacy. To be sure, there are particular moral and political issues where we are uncertain and admit to it, but there are other issues where we have strong convictions, even while acknowledging that some disagree with us and feel just as passionately about what they believe as we do about what we believe. Nevertheless, we hold to our convictions and judge those who disagree with us to be mistaken. You believe in liberal democracy; there are those on this planet who disagree. You believe in religious liberty (as conceived of in the West); there are those who disagree. You believe in government-funded universal health care; there are those who disagree. You believe in amnesty for undocumented workers; there are those who disagree. You are pro-life; there are those who disagree. You can come up with your own list and arrange it any way you like (my examples are chosen at random). It will probably be a long list, and for each item on it there will be those who disagree with you. They have their convictions and commitments, and you have yours.

Part of losing one's innocence about life is acquiring a deep awareness that we live in a world of competing political ideologies, moral perspectives, and religious visions advanced often, if not always, by thoughtful individuals and groups. It is in this kind of a world that God has placed us, the very world in which we are called to make our own commitments and to live them out in our lives. If we refuse to make any commitments or if no strong convictions capture our hearts and minds because we have encountered people who believe differently than we do, then we will become mere ciphers. There will be nothing substantial about us, no moral, political, or religious fiber. The point is that disagreement, even with good people, must not prevent commitment nor serve to empty us of all our strong convictions.

Yet we might reasonably conclude from the fact that there are people, not just ignorant and corrupt people, who disagree with us that we ought to hold our commitments more tentatively and be more restrained in our claim to possess the truth. Certainly "epistemological modesty," as it is sometimes called, is a virtue. We ought to have the capacity to be self-critical, to recognize our own fallibility, to listen to what others who disagree with us have to say, to be willing to take a second look at what we ourselves believe, and so forth. This seems obviously right, for who wants to be an arrogant know-it-all? But there are dangers lurking in the call to be modest and tentative in what we believe. G. K. Chesterton once observed, "Everyday one comes across somebody who says that of course his view may not be the right one. Of course his view must be the right one, or it is not his view. We are on the road to producing a race of men too mentally modest to believe in the multiplication table. . . . Scoffers of old times were too proud to be convinced; but these are too humble to be convinced."[2] Chesterton is quite correct in his analysis of what it is to hold a view or, what amounts to the same thing, to have a belief. For the concept of having a belief entails (there is no way around it) that I also believe that those beliefs incompatible with mine are false and those who hold them are mistaken. Even in changing my beliefs I recognize that I was mistaken in what I once believed and therefore those who believe what I once believed are also mistaken. This is simply what it is to have a belief. It would seem, absent some explanation, that those who look askance at religious believers who think that other religious believers are mistaken in what they believe (or some of what they believe) fail to understand what it is to have a belief. To be sure, some beliefs are held more tentatively than others. But to have a belief at all, it must at least be the case that one believes one's belief is more likely to be true than false, which in turn means that I believe I am more likely to be correct in what I believe than those who disagree with me, even should I admit I could be wrong.

Chesterton's comments capture something of the

2. Gilbert K. Chesterton, *Orthodoxy* (New York: Doubleday, 1990), p. 32.

spirit of our own age as well as his (early-twentieth-century), and provide a needed warning that there should be limits to any epistemological modesty. At some point such modesty can become a vice; one can become too intellectually tentative, and tentative about the wrong things. If we become too modest we simply won't have any beliefs at all, lacking the confidence to say (at least to ourself), "I am (likely) right and they are (likely) wrong." It is significant, however, that the call to epistemological modesty is more often than not directed at the person with strong religious convictions, not at the person with strong moral or political convictions. The latter two typically get a free pass. They apparently have no need for intellectual modesty nor for sermons extolling the virtue of self-doubt. These are reserved for the confident religious believer. This reflects a certain bias against religious belief that may be prompted by a fear of religion as a potentially destructive and divisive force. If religious beliefs are less confidently held, it might be thought, then religion's presence in the world will be less dangerous. (But also, one might add, it would be less of a force for good.) But even granting, as one must, the potential danger of perverted religious belief, one must also acknowledge the enormous potential danger of a perverted moral vision or a perverted political system. It is by no means obvious that strong religious convictions pose the greater potential danger. The one is no more likely to go astray and cause great evil than the other. Modesty of belief, therefore, is no more called for in the religious sphere than it is in the political or moral spheres where we unapologetically make strong commitments, have robust convictions, and are enthusiastic advocates for what we believe.

One reason some individuals, even within the Christian fold, are hesitant to embrace the strong truth claims associated with traditional Christianity is that they think, mistakenly, this automatically shuts the door of salvation to all those outside the Christian tradition who may not believe those truth claims nor even be acquainted with them. The issue of salvation (who is finally redeemed and who is not), however, is a different issue from the one discussed here. For one can with complete consistency affirm both the unique saving truth claims of Christianity and that those outside the Christian faith can and will be redeemed. They will ultimately come — somehow or other — to embrace Jesus, God's Son, as their Lord and Savior. So nothing said here about the truth claims of Christianity prejudices the salvation issue one way or the other. One can even be cautiously agnostic about it all. The full spectrum of views on this topic continues to be open to us.

In the larger culture the tendency to chide those with confident religious beliefs but not those with confident political or moral beliefs is in part the product of a certain kind of person who inhabits the world of religion but not, so far as I am aware, the moral and political worlds. Simone Weil describes these chiders as those who "think they are capable of impartiality because they have only a vague religiosity which they can turn indifferently in any direction."[3] But the last thing in the world we should want is a vague religiosity, any more than we should want a vague morality or a vague politics that we can turn indifferently in any direction. Such an attitude is incompatible with serious commitment, which always involves choosing from among the available options. You can't have them all — you have to choose. As Chesterton put it, "When you choose anything you reject everything else."[4] In the moral and political arenas strong commitment is taken for granted, and our culture recognizes that one who embraces a particular political or moral perspective is rejecting the other alternatives and becoming an advocate for that perspective. We should not be averse to a similar attitude in the religious sphere. None of this, however, precludes civil and respectful treatment of those who disagree with us, and the recognition that we can learn from them. Add to civility and respect a good infusion of love, and we need not be embarrassed for having strong, life-transforming religious convictions that we believe to be true.

Those undergoing existential doubt do not hold a "vague religiosity which they can turn indifferently in any direction." Nor, hopefully, will this be the end result of their struggle with doubt and uncertainty. Rather, it is hoped, they will see that robust commitments and confi-

3. Simone Weil, *Waiting for God* (New York: Harper and Row, 1973), p. 184.

4. Chesterton, *Orthodoxy*, p. 36.

dent beliefs can flourish and ought to flourish even in a world where (to echo Pascal) those beliefs are disputed and very many people deny them. It is also a world, we should never forget, in which "very many people" *affirm* them and confidently confess that "Jesus Christ is Lord."

QUESTIONS FOR REFLECTION

1. Has either your personal encounter with people who disagree with your basic Christian beliefs or your knowledge that the world is filled with such people induced uncertainty or tentativeness in you about your beliefs? If the answer is yes, why do you think it had that impact on you? Should it have that impact?

2. Are your moral and political beliefs less threatened by disagreement than are your religious beliefs? If so, why? Should they be?

13

*Why Not All Smart People Reject
What You Believe*

*Why Smart People Who Do Reject
What You Believe Isn't a Good Reason
for Joining Them*

The faith of Christian believers can be seriously challenged when they find themselves surrounded by exceptionally bright and intellectually able people who disagree with them. The challenge is especially acute when those believers respect the life of the mind. These bright and able souls that the believer respects may be utterly indifferent to religious belief or simply dismissive, maybe even hostile. Such an environment sounds very much like the typical secular college or university. Indeed, of all the social institutions in this land of ours, universities are the most secular when measured by such standards as belief in the existence of God and the embrace of a religious vision of life. It is not that one will necessarily be confronted by sophisticated antitheistic or antireligious arguments in such an environment, though that can happen. Rather, the challenge is more atmospheric and psychological than it is rigorously intellectual. It consists of antireligious attitudes expressed through humor and informal asides. There is the widespread operative assumption that religious truth claims are somehow intellectually retrograde, an assumption seldom argued for, simply assumed. In such an environment a religious person with a deep belief in God can feel bereft of adequate intellectual support. One is simply outnumbered and intellectually outgunned. Most academics, however, apart from small pockets of specialists, are not sophisticated about religious matters in the same way they are about political matters. Politics is, after all, the religion of the academy, and sophistication in this arena is not limited to specialists as it tends to be with religion. Indeed, many academics are relatively innocent about religion, not having been religious at any point during their intellectual maturity. To be sure, some may look back to a time when they were altar boys in the Roman Catholic Church or attended Sunday school at the local Baptist church or were bar mitzvahed at the synagogue, but there is often not much beyond that by way of religious understanding or even interest. Nevertheless, with all their varying degrees of comprehension, the critics are many and may pose a disturbing challenge for Christian believers, a challenge constituted by their sheer number alone. And they are bright, after all. Here I am reminded of a scene in a movie that takes place just before a battle between a large army of Puritan Roundheads (Cromwell's forces) and a smaller royalist army, fighting for Charles I. A rather effete and pudgy-looking nobleman on horseback, looking at the large enemy force, swallows hard and exclaims, "Oh, there are so many of them!" And seriously committed Christian believers may look around at an intellectual environment not at all sympathetic to what they believe, swallow hard, and utter those same words. Indeed, the intellectual forces arrayed against their beliefs appear to be legion.

There may be many of them, but matters are not quite as bleak as our religious believer may at first think. In fact, we may currently be experiencing the greatest revival of theistic philosophy (a defense of belief in God's existence along with some considerable support for traditional Christian doctrine) since the eighteenth century. As evidence, let me cite a nontheist philosopher, Quentin Smith, who is calling his fellow naturalists (i.e., those who deny the supernatural and affirm that all reality can ultimately be explained by the natural sciences) to rise to the defense of their naturalism against the recent attacks by theistic philosophers.[1] The naturalists, he tells us, have been receiving a good old-fashioned philosophical drubbing. The theists have succeeded, he admits, in defeating the arguments that have been advanced in favor of naturalism and naturalists are no longer justified in holding their beliefs. Smith, in this article, is attempting to rally his

[1]. Quentin Smith, "The Metaphilosophy of Naturalism," *Philo* 4, no. 2 (2001). The following quotations are from this article.

troops to confront this theistic onslaught and to restore a justification for naturalism. In his rallying call he refers to the "erudite brilliance of theistic philosophizing today" and cites a reliable estimate that one-fourth to one-third of all philosophy professors are currently theists, "most being orthodox Christians." Think of that. Not bad to have a little firepower on your side. Just to know it's there gives the lie to the claim that the really bright and able people uniformly reject religion and theism. In fact, in the academy, these people think far more about the rationality of religious belief than does the average academic.

Moreover, the activity of these philosophers has resulted in an explosion of books defending theistic belief. Smith writes, "A count could show that in Oxford University Press' 2000-2001 catalog, there are 96 recently published books on the philosophy of religion (94 advancing theism and 2 presenting 'both sides')." This is by no means true of general introductory texts in philosophy, however, where the attitude toward theism is not quite so positive, but in the specialized area of philosophy of religion there is a theistic dominance. Smith writes, "If each naturalist who does not specialize in the philosophy of religion (i.e., over ninety-nine percent of naturalists) were locked in a room with theists who do specialize in the philosophy of religion, and if the ensuing debate were refereed by a naturalist who had a specialization in the philosophy of religion . . . I expect the most probable outcome is that the naturalist, wanting to be a fair and objective referee, would have to conclude that the theists definitely had the upper hand in every single argument or debate." Smith concludes that no longer will "a hand waving dismissal of theism" by naturalist philosophers suffice, which is "like trying to halt a tidal wave with a hand-held sieve." But in the larger academy there is a considerable amount of confident (overly confident, as it turns out) dismissive hand waving. A Christian believer can be overcome with uncertainty by such hand waving without ever being exposed to serious, credible, sustained arguments. But it doesn't always take arguments. A bit of hand-waving dismissal by academically respectable people often does the job quite nicely. We are, after all, all of us, impressionable creatures. None of us is completely immune to such hand waving. One can begin to appreciate the observation that removing oneself from the grip of the hand wavers is more like breaking a spell than following a complicated argument to its conclusion, though one should not be afraid of complicated arguments.

Well, what should we think about all this? It's not that the religious believer should run to the nearest philosophy department and expect to be greeted with open arms. That won't happen. Nor should graduates go back to college and get a second major in philosophy. The point here is a simple one: not all the very best minds are on the other side. Far from it. And there are other academic disciplines where able practitioners of their craft affirm a thoughtful, knowledgeable, and morally sensitive commitment to the gospel of Jesus Christ. Though there is a historical ebb and flow in these matters, right now at the most technical philosophical level theists probably do have the upper hand, or at least are holding their own. And that is encouraging.

Fifty years ago, if I can play the role of the historian for a moment, the social environment in the United States was deferential toward religious belief and warmly embracing. Angry public attacks on Christianity were rare to nonexistent, and strong expressions of religious skepticism were considered beyond the pale in most communities. There were no books on the *New York Times* bestseller list (or its equivalent) that attacked religion and belief in God. In the rarefied climes of the academy matters were quite different, especially in the discipline of philosophy where defenders of theism were few and far between. Skepticism and naturalism prevailed with no significant opposition. Today, fifty years later, there has been a curious reversal. One feels much freer to attack religious belief in public, in editorials and books aimed at a broad audience. And in recent years, a spate of books hostile to religion and belief in God has appeared. Whereas in the professional philosophical community, as we have just seen, God has been doing quite well. So while not all smart people believe in God, you can take comfort that many do, especially in an area where such belief would not be casual or unthinking.

∞∞∞

QUESTIONS FOR REFLECTION

1. Is there a basic respect for the academic world in your church and among people you associate with? Or is that world somehow suspect? If so, why? Do you agree with this?

2. Which poses the greater challenge for you: the existence of intellectually able people who reject *all* religious belief (a secular humanist, say) or the existence of sincere people who are of a different religion than yours?

14

Why Christians Aren't Always as Good as Non-Christians

Why God Still Gets the Credit

Why Christians Should Applaud Goodness Wherever They Find It

Mahatma Gandhi, the great liberator of India, is said to have remarked that the only thing wrong with Christianity is the Christians. To be sure, we Christians are sometimes a rather dismal lot. It is not that Gandhi found the ideals of the Gospels wanting but that the Christians who espoused them too often fell woefully short of those ideals. And as challenging as Gandhi's words may be, we are even challenged more when we personally encounter non-Christians who are morally admirable in so many ways. Indeed, they seem to be better people than many in the Christian community, ourselves included. They may be people of a different religion or of no religion at all, and we find in them much to be admired. But why is it, we may wonder, that non-

Christians can have virtues that some genuine Christians lack and some genuine Christians have vices that some non-Christians are free of? Why aren't we of the Christian faith always and in all ways better than those who do not know Christ or at least do not know him in his fullness?

When we look around at the world in which we live — and we don't have to look very far — and view all the various and sundry beliefs that people hold and the different kinds of people there are and the varying circumstances that have shaped their lives, the variety that confronts us is staggering. There are the rich and the poor, the educated and the illiterate, the criminal and the law abider, the socialist and the libertarian, the liberal and the conservative, the lazy and the industrious, the heavy drinker and the teetotaler, the gang member and the Boy Scout, the well organized and the scatterbrained, the smart and the intellectually struggling, the jock and the nerd, the short-tempered and the patient, the foolish and the wise, just to name a small, random selection of people who inhabit our planet and our neighborhood. And it is into just this kind of world that God in Christ came and calls all peoples to himself, people in their infinite variety. The gospel is for all of them, and from each of these categories, and many, many more, they have come, bringing with them all that they are, both the good and the bad, their strengths and their weaknesses, their virtues and their vices. They come, not always in morally tip-top condition. There are the short-tempered, the opinionated, the unimaginative, the snobbish, the shallow, the gullible, the grumpy, the insecure, the stubborn, the self-pitying, the small-minded — just for starters. They all come, and they come with vices big and small. They come for forgiveness and a new life. They come reaching out for something that they themselves don't fully comprehend, as none of us do when we begin the journey of faith. All of us are in for some surprises along the way.

We are very much like individuals going to college who want to be intellectually deepened and enlarged. We have an inkling of what is involved, but only as we are actually deepened and enlarged does it become clear what we had been wanting and reaching out for all along. So it is with Christian converts. They come seeking something that has to do with accepting God's love and forgiveness, manifesting that love and forgiveness in their own lives, and following Jesus and becoming more like him. Granted that these are powerful and transforming inklings, but they are nevertheless only inklings. With time and growth these new Christians will begin to see more clearly what this all means and the implications it has for their own lives. For all of us in the early stages of our faith journey, there is so much we do not grasp, so many faults and weaknesses in our lives that we do not even recognize. It all takes time. Moreover, some individuals are morally better off when they start their Christian journey, while others lag behind and have some catching up to do. It is inevitable that some Christians will end up struggling with weaknesses and vices that some non-Christians are free of. This is because some bring to Christ faults that those who do not come do not have.

To take but one example: from the group of humans struggling with anger management some will hear and respond to the gospel message, while from the group of humans fortunate enough not to have such problems, some will not respond to the gospel message or will not have the opportunity to do so. The result is, some Christians with anger management issues and some non-Christians totally free of them. In that regard the non-Christian is better than, as well as better off than, the Christian — judged even by standards that the Christian community itself recognizes and honors. Similar cases abound. This is one reason why Christians can often learn from non-Christians. And all this is a result of the vast diversity in the kinds of individuals who populate our world and have responded to the gospel invitation. The call of Christ goes out to all, and it is for all. We can't then complain when all kinds of people — warts and all — respond.

When people do come to Christ, perfection is not achieved instantaneously (nor is it ever achieved in this life). If it were, then all Christians would indeed be better than all non-Christians. We would be perfect, and they would not. Alas, we are not perfect. To be sure, in some instances the initial changes in a person who embraces the gospel are dramatic and inspiring. This is often so in cases where the vices are especially egregious. Thus, the gang member turns his back on his old way of life, the criminal goes straight, the irresponsible and abusive husband becomes the caring husband he should have been, the addict overcomes her addiction, and so forth. These kinds of transformations are not uncommon and testify to the power of the gospel to change lives in a dramatic and positive fashion. But even this is not perfection achieved, for there remains a range of less obvious faults and vices that these radically changed individuals continue to confront, as we all do. The process of moral and spiritual transformation is, after all, a lifelong project. The theological name for this is "sanctification."

The test to which we should put the genuineness of conversion is not whether the Christian convert is better than non-Christians but, as Lewis proposes, whether the person who comes to Christ is better than she would have been had she not come.[1] One becomes a new creation, moving in a new direction, best summed up as loving God with all one's heart, soul, and mind, and one's neighbor as oneself. It's not that we do either of these with anything approaching perfection or even full understanding, but we do acquire a new sense that this is what we are called to be, and deep down it is what we want to be, lovers of God and neighbor. We have at least begun the process of transformation, and some of us, it so happens, have a lot further to go than others.

The adequacy of the Christian faith and our confi-

1. C. S. Lewis, *Mere Christianity* (San Francisco: HarperCollins, 2001), p. 210.

dence in it, however, should be a product less of whether or not Christians are always morally better than non-Christians and more of appreciating the rich context within which Christians, with all their faults and limitations, are called to engage in the project of moral and spiritual transformation. It is a context provided by the Christian church, the fellowship of believers, the teaching of Scripture, the doctrinal formulations of the great creeds, and the presence of the Holy Spirit. This nurturing environment is at the heart of the Christian faith, and it brings with it a range of convictions to support this new way of life. Crucially, it is firmly believed that the difference between right and wrong, good and evil, virtue and vice is deep and significant. More specifically, the difference between love and hate, kindness and cruelty, justice and injustice is not simply one of personal or group preference; rather, there exist moral norms grounded in the character of a loving, holy, just, and eternal God. The difference between good and evil matters, and it matters deeply.

This fundamental conviction makes possible something crucial for the moral life, namely, *moral seriousness:* taking moral issues seriously, working hard at them, trying to determine what's right, because it's important to know what's right and do what's right. One response to a moral quandary is not as good as any other, as it would be on the personal preference view. The conviction that there is a real right and wrong provides a foundation and incentive to work hard at the moral issues that confront us. A word of caution is warranted here, however. Just because there is an objective right and wrong, it does not follow that we who believe there is have all the answers to all the perplexing questions that confront us both in the public arena and in our personal lives, nor does it follow that we see with perfect clarity what true moral goodness looks like and how it is to manifest itself in our lives. It is one thing to believe there is a right answer to a question, and it is quite another to believe you have that answer. But belief in an objective right and wrong does provide a firm basis for taking the moral life seriously. It also makes possible *moral resolve:* doing what is right even when it is highly demanding to do so, even when substantial sacrifice is called for because doing what's right and being the right kind of person are that important.

Moreover, because moral standards are grounded in a personal Being, we find ourselves accountable to Someone for what we do and what we become. To this personal Being we are to come regularly for self-examination, repentance, forgiveness, and renewal. We are all the while being challenged by a compelling moral ideal, self-giving love modeled in the person of Jesus. And this Christian ethic of love, as Reinhold Niebuhr observed, because it is an impossible ethic (no matter how much we love, we can always love more), is always relevant. We never get to the top of the mountain and look around for new moral challenges, new mountains to conquer. We are not the moral analogues of Alexander the Great, who lamented that there were no more empires for him to conquer. Further, grateful to God for creating and redeeming us, followers of Christ seek to do what is right and loving, not only because it is right and loving but also because it is pleasing to God. Moral acts are at the deepest level acts of gratitude. They are never viewed as means of securing salvation, which would turn the moral life into a self-serving project, but rather are expressions of gratitude for a salvation already freely given to us in Jesus Christ. And it is the presence and activity of God's Spirit that enable the person of faith to bring more and more regions of thought, feelings, character, and action under the sway of Christ and his love. What better context for the moral development of sinful and struggling but spiritually aspiring followers of Christ? So, yes, we regret that we Christians are often not all we should be (though we should not forget that there are those who are much closer to the Christian ideal than we are and who provide us with inspiring models of deep faith and moral goodness), but here the suggestion is not to look only at Christians with their faults and shortcomings but also to look with an appreciative eye at this sanctifying and transforming context that we are invited to be a part of.

In this big world of ours, it soon becomes obvious that we not only confront *able* people who see things differently than we do, but we also encounter *good* people who see things differently than we do. We should not be taken aback by the presence of this goodness nor resent it, but rejoice and thank God for it. After all, God makes this goodness possible. This is the famous doctrine of "common grace." God is at work in the world at large, enabling good things to happen. This is grace that is "common," operating beyond the boundaries of the Christian church. Thus, Paul tells us that there are Gentiles who, although they do not have the law, nevertheless keep the law (Rom. 2:14-15). Outside the biblical tradition, he implicitly acknowledges, there can be found that which is true, noble, right, pure, lovely, excellent, and praiseworthy (Phil. 4:8). God recognizes, Scripture tells us, that those without the gospel can fear God, be devout, give graciously to the poor, and do what is right (Acts 10:1-3, 30-31, 34-36). And what God recognizes, we should recognize. Therefore, we are to respect other cultures, peoples, and religions, rejoicing in the truth they discover, the beauty they create, and the goodness they manifest. We are not to withhold our applause because they are not "one of us." Nevertheless, measured by the standard of God's holiness, we are all sinners, even those we applaud. All of us are in need of God's forgiveness and loving embrace despite the relative goodness that we (hopefully) and others manifest. Thus the gospel of the life, death, and resurrection of Jesus Christ is of supreme importance for all of humanity. So we rejoice in the good things we see in the world, wherever they are found and in whomever they are found, recognizing that there is also much sin, evil, and depravity, all the while commending to one and all the unique redemption that comes from God through Jesus Christ.

QUESTIONS FOR REFLECTION

1. How has your understanding of what it means to be a follower of Jesus Christ deepened and changed over the years? Can you be specific?

2. Do you know non-Christians (people belonging either to another religious tradition or to no faith tradition at all) who impress you by their "goodness" and spiritual seriousness? Does this perplex and challenge you in any way?

3. How does a Christian vision of life and its meaning deepen and enrich your understanding of the moral life? How do you think your moral life would differ if you lacked a belief in God?

15

Why God Doesn't Make His Presence More Obvious

Why We Need to Come to Terms with This

The theologian J. S. Whale began a series of eight lectures at Cambridge University with these words:

> [A]ll lectures on Christian doctrine are concerned from first to last with the reality, nature and purpose of the living God.
>
> But is there a God? Apparently not. God is not apparent to our senses. Nor is he indubitably apparent to human reason.[1]

If Whale is correct in saying that it is not obvious that there is a God, then, assuming there is a God, as Whale himself devoutly believed, why didn't God make his existence undeniably obvious? Why the obscurity? Though most people (past and present) have believed in some

---

1. J. S. Whale, *Christian Doctrine* (London: Fontana Books, 1957), p. 11.

form of a divine reality, there is a history of genuine debate on the topic of God's existence. This consists of a continuing series of arguments and counterarguments. In our Western world it has been "parry and thrust" since the eighteenth century. Certainly there have been and continue to be able defenders of the claim that God exists, but there have also been able critics. So why hasn't God made his existence so obvious that no one in his right mind would deny it? The mere fact that some feel compelled to defend the existence of God with arguments is itself an admission that God's existence is not like that of the Golden Gate Bridge or Mount Everest, the existence of which no one challenges and no one sees any need to defend. They are just there, and they are obviously, undeniably there. An announced debate on the topic "Does the Golden Gate Bridge Exist?" would not draw much of a crowd on a university campus, unless students were tweaked by curiosity and attended on a lark. Not so, should the debate be over the existence of God. Here the matter is not only vitally important but also debatable.

Robert Ingersoll, the famous nineteenth-century skeptic, purportedly challenged the claim that there is a God by calling out to the heavens, "If there is a God, I dare this God to strike me dead in the next 60 seconds." Ingersoll would then count out the seconds: "60, 59, 58, 57 . . . 0." When the minute was up, Ingersoll, still alive, would then address the assembled crowd: "See, my friends, there is no God." One might wonder, why didn't

God oblige? A bolt of lightning would have done quite nicely. Or possibly in a more benign demonstration of his presence, God might simply pick up Ingersoll, toss him high into the air, twist him, turn him, and somersault him for a good 60 seconds, finally returning him gently and safely to good old terra firma, accompanied by a loud voice, "Be well assured, Robert Ingersoll, I most certainly do exist." I suspect that would have done the job. Further, all atheists, agnostics, and those wavering in their faith might be subjected to similar but possibly less frightening demonstrations. Or why could God not have such a pervasive presence throughout this planet of ours, so powerful and undeniable, that all people at all times would not only believe but actually know beyond a shadow of a doubt that God exists, just as people who drive across the Golden Gate Bridge on a daily basis know beyond a shadow of a doubt that the bridge exists? If it is crucially important that we come to know God and to continue in our faith journey once begun, as Christians believe, then why has God not made his presence undeniable? The person of faith struggling with doubt and uncertainty may, for one, want a divine incursion so powerful and undeniable that all doubt and uncertainty will be swept away in one brief moment. Surely an all-powerful God could make his existence undeniable for all people, including all our doubters. But he has not done this. Why not?

The reason may have something to do with God wanting to provide a context that will enable us to say no as well as yes to his overtures. There may be other reasons for this obscurity, but this is, I believe, one of them. But, first, why is our capacity to say no to God so important? Because it is the possibility of no that invests the ultimate yes with significance. Consider a man (here we will be traditionalists for a moment) proposing marriage to a woman. A pretty scary prospect, this — scary for the man, who is quite vulnerable on such an occasion. He not only declares his love but also offers himself as a lifelong partner. For the woman to reject the offer, even if done gently, is not merely to reject a proposal. It is to reject the man, the one making the proposal. And that hurts. Suppose, however, that with advanced technology and the help of some devious friends who are also scientific geniuses, the man places an electrode in the brain of the beloved (unbeknownst to her), programming her so that she will respond just as he wishes. Now a yes is guaranteed, all risk of a rejection is eliminated, and no blow to the man's ego is possible. With electrode in place, the suitor can now breathe easy. Thus the proposal is made and the inevitable yes is given in response. The suitor may want more than a yes. He may also ask for declarations of his beloved's love that, with the aid of the electrode and the push of a button, will be forthcoming with considerable effusiveness: "You are the most wonderful man God has ever created. I am so lucky. I do love you so." But what does this all amount to? Clearly, not much. The yes, engineered as it is by the suitor, is emptied of significance. Gone is the capacity to say no, and with it goes any signif-

138

icance attaching to the yes. In theological terms, God is the suitor and we are the ones being sought. But God has a problem, if we can be so bold to put it in those terms. The problem is this: How can God be sufficiently present so that we can know of his existence and therefore be able to hear and respond to his proposal, but not be so overwhelmingly present, as with Ingersoll's somersaults through the air, that he makes it impossible for us to reject him? How is this via media to be achieved?

To underscore the challenge, think of a somewhat analogous problem confronting children raised in the home of a strong-willed, exceptionally talented father, one with a dominating personality. Think perhaps of a Winston Churchill or someone with comparable gifts and force of presence. The child may be so overwhelmed by the father that he becomes a mere echo of this dominant and gifted man. The child raised in such a household may find it nigh unto impossible to shape a life of his own, becoming a mere extension of the "great man." To continue to live under the same roof may doom any prospect for meaningful autonomy. To secure some measure of independence, the child may have to distance himself from his father. After he has done so for a sufficient period of time and established a life of his own, the values the child then affirms and embraces will be his own, whether or not they are the same as those of his father. If one can begin to appreciate the threat that such a talented and dominant father poses for the child's independence, think how much greater is the threat posed by a God whose unveiled power and glory would be overwhelming. It would be an infinitely greater threat, crushing all possibility of free agency, rendering a no an impossibility. This God who possesses all virtues, all perfection, all power, all glory, and beside whom all human greatness is but a faint shadow, would overwhelm his creatures unless he in some way or other veils himself, rendering his presence less obvious, more obscure. And this, I am suggesting, is just what God has done.

This is not to deny that miraculous interventions occur in our lives, a healing perhaps or special direction through an improbable conjunction of events, but these are not occurrences that one is forced to attribute to divine power. For it is one thing to be cured of cancer in ways inexplicable by science, where one could still insist, should one so choose, that if only we knew enough the event could be explained completely by natural causes. It is something quite different to have amputees sprouting new limbs in front of astonished onlookers or for the deceased at a funeral to get up out of the coffin and return home with the rejoicing family. In the latter two cases one would be hard pressed to explain away what had happened in purely naturalistic terms. Here there would be no room for doubt, no wiggle room for unbelief. A naturalistic explanation would seem to be definitively ruled out. Thus even with the miraculous, God typically gives us freedom not to believe should that be our strong inclination. For this reason we don't have miracles involving sprouting limbs nor resurrections at funerals. Nevertheless, there may be some contexts, rare perhaps, where a more dramatic and less discreet incursion of divine power would actually be liberating and not intimidating. These are miracles that actually free people to say yes. One could imagine situations where dark and very powerful supernatural forces are at work, oppressing and tyrannizing. In such a context it is possible that only a divine counterforce, powerful and dramatic, could break the chains of such malevolent powers, freeing a person to believe. It is God in his sovereign judgment that determines when the miraculous is to occur, and then how powerful and apparent the interventions should be. God does the calibrating in ways appropriate to the particular occasion. But in the world in which we live, these interventions are typically discreet and restrained, open to alternative explanations and requiring the eyes of faith, be it the faith and vision of the naturalist or the faith and vision of the supernaturalist.

Though God does not force himself upon us with an undeniable presence, that does not mean that God has left us bereft of reasons to believe in his existence. There is evidence, even if it is not indisputable evidence. Perhaps a more helpful word than "evidence" is "clue." God has left us with clues that point to his existence, and one of the interesting features about a clue is that it can be overlooked or misread. Consider the following example. Suppose I am out with a group of friends and I'm in a rather loquacious mood, chattering away about a range of matters. My wife leans over the table across from me, stares at me intently, and clears her throat. It suddenly occurs to me that she is trying to alert me to something, and then it dawns on me that I am making public some matters that are better left private. After this episode I may not be able to convince a friend who witnessed this that my wife was cautioning me about my disclosures. My friend insists that my wife leaned forward and stared intently because she was interested in what I was saying; she cleared her throat for the same reason we all clear our throats. So there we have it: one set of clues but two interpretations. I can't convince my friend, but I'm sure I'm right, and as it turns out, I am.

The clues God has left us are multiple. There is the extraordinary fact of the universe. It doesn't have to exist but there it is, and moreover, our planet is inhabited by so many wonderful things: dinosaurs and tigers, palm trees and roses, whales and humans. Then there is the uniformity of nature, not a chaos but unvaried patterns and regularities that obtain throughout the whole of the universe; whether we are on the planet Earth or in the furthest reaches of space, the same laws of nature apply. Then there is the moral order, our sense that we are accountable to something beyond ourselves, a standard of right and wrong that transcends the human community. It is natural to read all these as clues pointing to a creator God. But then, of course, there is a dark side as well: pain, disease, suffering, and death. This may give us pause and create considerable ambiguity. But this mixed picture may be understood as a fitting context for a test of the heart. What is it that we want to be true? For it is not just our cognitive abilities but the desires of our heart that play a part in moving us in one direction or the other. As Pascal put it, "There is enough light for those who desire only to see, and enough darkness for those of a contrary disposition."[2]

QUESTIONS FOR REFLECTION

1. Most Christians have not personally experienced incursions of divine power so dramatic and overwhelming that they compel belief, not merely prompt or encourage belief. Is that also true for you and for those you have known?

2. Could it be that powerful displays of divine power might in some contexts and cultures be intimidating (forcing belief) but in other contexts and cultures liberating (opening one to the possibility of belief)?

3. How important is it that you and I have the freedom to say no to God? How have we in our own lives said no to God, even if this was not an ultimate or definitive no?

2. Blaise Pascal, *Pensées* (London: Penguin Books, 1966), #149.

16

Why Wintry Spiritual Types Can Be Profoundly Spiritual

Why the Seasonal Nature of the Spiritual Life Brings Us Both Winter and Summer

When going through those dark patches in our Christian journey, we still need to maintain a meaningful spiritual life. Some may wonder, however, whether there can be a genuine spirituality — deep and meaningful — for those plagued by doubt and uncertainty, agonizing as they are over the absence of God. If this is a quickly passing phase, there is not much to be concerned about. However, if matters are prolonged, what then are the possibilities? Here we need to reflect on and embrace a different kind of spirituality, but a real spirituality all the same.

Martin Marty has observed that the imagery associated with the Christian journey of faith has tended to be spatial imagery — pilgrims moving along a road toward a heavenly city, some portions of the road pleasant, the scenery pleasing and progress rapid, other portions of the road rocky, mountainous, and demanding. The point is to keep moving, to reach one's destination, the heavenly city. The classic exposition using this imagery is, of course, John Bunyan's *Pilgrim's Progress*. Marty suggests that there is another image, temporal and seasonal, rather than spatial, that may also help illuminate features of the spiritual life: summer and winter.[1] Summer is a time of foot-stomping spiritual exuberance. God is close. God is in control. Our spirits soar. These are the good times, free of doubt and uncertainty. It is unthinkable that God is not real, active in our world and in our lives. But then there is winter, the winter of the heart powerfully captured, as we have seen, by John Crowe Ransom:

A cry of Absence, Absence in the heart
And in the wood the furious winter blowing.[2]

This too is a season of the spiritual year, winter being as much a seasonal reality as summer.

To experience the winter of the heart, as most do, at least to some degree and at some point in their lives, does not constitute an automatic departure from a vital spirituality, as if such a spirituality were the exclusive possession of those basking in the sunshine of the summer

1. Martin E. Marty, *A Cry of Absence* (San Francisco: Harper and Row, 1983), pp. 1-21.
2. Quoted in Marty, *A Cry of Absence*, p. 1.

months. It is rather a call to a different kind of spirituality, possibly a deeper and certainly a more demanding spirituality, but a spirituality all the same. Marty observes that there are two types of spirituality: summery and wintry spirituality; both have traditionally been present in the church and have found expression in its devotional literature. Neither one has privileged standing over against the other, and neither one is (as Marty puts it, borrowing from Karl Rahner) "chemically pure," completely isolated from the other. The summer of faith and the winter of faith are experienced by most of us, but for some (and Marty is apparently putting himself in this category) the winter of the heart is a season that never completely disappears. But even here the inbreaking of warmth is not precluded. Thaws come even to those of a chillier spiritual temperament.

Nevertheless, despite the wintry conditions, there can be (all the same) a profound devotion, a deep love of God, and an impressive faithfulness. For wintry spirituality calls for a special kind of devotion — a kind of wrestling with God that we find in certain portions of Scripture, especially, but not only, in the psalms of lament.

> My God, my God, why have you forsaken me?
> > Why are you so far from helping me, from the
> > > words of my groaning?
> O my God, I cry by day, but you do not answer;
> > and by night, but find no rest.

(Ps. 22:1-2 NRSV)

This represents an impressive spirituality. Here there is a dogged faithfulness — a commitment to wrestle with God rather than abandon the relationship even when God appears to be silent and remote. It is a spirituality that does not seek false comfort or pretend that reality is other than it is. Yet, it is to the silent God that one turns, and it is with this God that one struggles. As Martin Marty observes, "Even the cry from the depths is an affirmation: Why cry if there is no hint or hope of hearing? Why not mutter to one's self, or sulk? The cry comes with no clear expectations, but it does imply a 'Thou.'"[3]

The outward life of faithful wintry Christians may not look much different from that of their summery fellows. They sit in the pew, listen to sermons, sing God's praises, and partake of the sacraments (or ordinances). They linger over passages of Scripture, especially certain passages in the Psalms that they feel speak to their condition. They understand that the church is a place where beliefs are affirmed, not doubts expressed, so they do not expect their uncertainties to take center stage. And they acknowledge that it is here that they find articulated their hopes, if not always their indubitable beliefs. They participate in the ministries of the church to reach out with love to a desperate and needy world, doing so in the name of Christ. And as they mature in their understanding of their own situation (past or present), they feel called to a ministry of understanding, seeking to provide fellowship and hope to

3. Marty, *A Cry of Absence*, p. 120.

those who share the winter they have known. Where they themselves once cried out, silently perhaps, for understanding, they now seek to respond to similar cries from others. They seek to give the troubled heart what they themselves did not have — space to be heard and understood. Sometimes all it takes by way of a response is, "I've been there too." At least that's a start.

Here, however, we must be careful. It is possible for us to misread our own situation and wrongly criticize our worship and devotional practices because of a lack of feelings accompanying those activities. Here it may be that we are not so much experiencing the winter of the heart as making a transition, possibly as an aftermath of the dark night, to a more mature spirituality, one that is less feeling-dependent. We can mistakenly conclude that our worship and devotions are spiritually substandard because they lack what they had before the dark night of the soul descended upon us. The standard for worship becomes how it was before the dark night, and using that standard we judge our current worship to be deficient, even dead. But how it was before may not be how it should be now. And part of maturing is seeing how that is so.

John of the Cross once again proves helpful. He faults beginners in the faith for placing too much store on feelings. And beginners may not be alone in this regard. His words, wise and to the point, certainly have a contemporary relevance. "In receiving Communion they spend all their time trying to get some feelings and satisfaction rather than humbly praising and reverencing God dwelling within them. And they go about this in such a way that, if they do not procure any sensible feeling and satisfaction, they think they have accomplished nothing."[4] It needs to be stressed that the absence of certain feelings does not mean that one's worship is not real or authentic. The object of worship is to honor and reverence God, not to seek and obtain certain feelings. And if I have done just that with my worship, I should rest content. Consider an analogous situation: an occasion honoring someone for a promotion or upon retirement. I may think highly of this person who is a good friend, am in attendance to honor her, and wouldn't miss it for all the world. Yet I may not be swept along by feelings or emotions. I may even have suffered from an unpleasant and distracting headache throughout the evening while a delicious meal was served and speeches lauding my friend were given. Yet at the end of this festive occasion, I return home content and satisfied that a good and honorable person had been appropriately honored and that I was privileged to be part of it. I was happy she was honored and glad for her, but I was glad for the occasion, not for the feelings that were, after all, derivative and secondary. The people present respected her and recognized her many virtues, and had gathered together for the sole purpose of giving expression to their esteem. They didn't attend seeking feelings, nor did they evaluate the success of the occasion by

4. *John of the Cross: Selected Writings,* ed. Kieran Kavanaugh (New York: Paulist, 1987), p. 175.

149

the presence of feelings and emotions. So it is with corporate worship. We have honored our God, paid our respects, and should feel privileged to have done so. That, and not feelings or emotions, is fundamental.

The danger of a feeling-dependent spirituality, as John of the Cross has pointed out, is that when those feelings abate or are absent in worship and prayer, new followers of Jesus (and old ones as well) can become "bored" with it all and either "give it up" or "go to it begrudgingly."[5] One is thereby falling victim to a feeling-based faith, rather than having a commitment-based faith that survives the ebb and flow of feelings. It's not that one would want a spirituality devoid of feelings — that would not be at all desirable. For there *will* be times when the heart is "strangely warmed," when we are deeply touched and greatly moved. But we should also recognize that devoted service and authentic worship do not require the invariable presence of those feelings that the beginner sees as the hallmark of authenticity.

Further, to raise a slightly different but related concern, one can mistakenly believe, encouraged by the positive and rapid changes that often occur during the early days of faith, that healthy spirituality will always move apace, accompanied by immediately evident signs of progress. This is what healthy spirituality is supposed to look like, and if that is not what is happening, then there is something wrong, we mistakenly conclude. Spiritual

5. *John of the Cross,* p. 177.

progress, it is thought, is always to be rapid and sustained. To the contrary, almost all important growth in a life, whether it be spiritual, mental, or physical, takes place so slowly, so gradually, indiscernible increment by indiscernible increment, that one is not even aware that it is taking place. But it is, and over time the transformation can be staggering. The twenty-inch baby becomes a six footer, but at no time is there any awareness of the growth that is occurring. One eats, one plays, and one grows. In time, that infant is the six footer. Consider intellectual growth, an even better analogy for our purposes. You enter kindergarten as a child with a child's mind. But when you graduate from high school thirteen years later, or from college seventeen years later, the intellectual transformation has been profound. Yet for most of us there were no (or at least very few) quantum leaps forward, nor was our educational experience attended by constant excitement. Even if some of us were a bit lackadaisical about it all and the transformation was not all that it might have been, nevertheless what a dramatic difference those years made in our lives. It just took time, we stayed with it, and we reaped the benefits: an adult mind.

So it is with spiritual growth. It is a product of long-term commitment to a process that involves worship, sermons, prayer, Scripture, hymns, fellowship, service, trials, temptations, and, importantly, life experience. One will seldom be aware of the growth as it is taking place. As with intellectual growth, so it is with spiritual transformation, it is achieved indiscernible increment by indiscernible increment. There is seldom short-term, measurable change or improvement that one can point to. Nevertheless, God's "invisible grace" is at work in our lives, and it works, as it typically does, in a manner that is slow and steady. It involves us in a routine faithfully followed over time. To be sure, there will be occasions when the spirit soars and the heart is deeply moved, maybe even some times when there is observable progress that we can point to, but that is not the only way God is at work in our lives, transforming us into the likeness of his Son. It is in fact only a small part of that transforming process. Typically it is slow and gradual, but all the same it is real and substantial.

But when we make this transition from an overdependence on feelings in our spiritual lives, we should move forward positively, aware that God is at work in our lives, moving us slowly and steadily closer to being the kind of person he would have us be. This is all quite consistent with a confidence in God's reality, a confidence free from the doubts, uncertainties, and agony of soul that is characteristic of that dark night and provides the somber undertones of a wintry spirituality. For a feeling- and emotion-driven spiritual life is not a necessary component of a strong confidence in God's reality, so its absence should not be disturbing to us, as with gratitude and joy we move forward in our spiritual journey.

Still, there are those of our number, and we may find ourselves among them, who are trying to be faithful amidst the dark night of the soul. For them it is a wintry spirituality, not merely one that is less feeling-dependent. Here there is "Absence in the heart" and a struggle to be true amidst polar conditions. Here the call is simply to be faithful. Certainly one of the advantages of the imagery of summer and winter for the spiritual life is that it rightly suggests to us that just as winter is a season of the weather, to be expected and prepared for, so winter is a season of the spiritual life, also to be expected and prepared for. Its occurrence should not surprise us, though its first occurrence often does. Normal spiritual life does involve summery and wintry times. Knowing this in advance is a valuable insight and helps prevent despair and the abandonment of faith. We do not cease to be spiritual, nor is there anything wrong with us when winter comes. Yes, winter comes, but so does summer. Summer is as real as winter. And when those wintry spiritual periods do come, we can anticipate, as we do with winter weather, the spring thaw and warmer days ahead. Such is the seasonal nature of the spiritual life. Wintry souls simply confess that this is where they find themselves at present and identify with the psalmist:

> I wait for the LORD, my soul waits, . . .
>   more than watchmen for the morning.
>
> (Ps. 130:5-6 RSV)

QUESTIONS FOR REFLECTION

1. If many of us have indeed experienced existential doubt and a sense of Absence, why have we in the church tended to be rather silent about it?

2. Did your worship experience at one time contain more of an emotional component than it does now? If so, was this change sudden or gradual? Did you ever judge that because of this you had lost something valuable, something essential to worship at its highest and best? If you did think that at one time, do you still think so now?

3. Reflect on the character of a wintry spirituality. Why is it a genuine form of spirituality rather than a lack of spirituality or a defective spirituality?

4. Reflect on those summery periods in your own Christian journey. What were they like?

17

Why Concluding Remarks Do Not Come Easily

Why the Dedication Page Finally Makes Sense

Why God Is Both Our Adversary and Our Ally

There is a genuine challenge in writing concluding remarks for a book that deals with existential doubt and the dark night of the soul, and does so with such brevity. For one thing, a summary of such a short book makes little sense. A quick glance at the table of contents should suffice. For another, to seek to highlight only the most important and helpful observations would be a highly subjective undertaking. Even among those who share the same faith, and are doctrinally and liturgically of the same mind, there may be significant differences, often rooted in variations in personality, temperament, and general mental outlook. We differ in so many ways: in our capacity to trust, in our ability to live with mystery, in our awareness of life's complexity, in the theological and biblical categories available to us, in how literal-minded we are or how developed are our poetic and metaphorical sensibilities, how sharpened are our analytic and logical skills, and so on. All these differences — and many others — shape our doubt when it comes and largely determine which responses to that doubt will be found helpful or even comprehensible.

But let me say this. A virtue that will prove helpful — one often in short supply — is patience, a willingness to carry through the wintry times in hope of summer and a more comforting presence in the days ahead. Or patience in adjusting to a new understanding of the nature of the spiritual life and our walk with God, one perhaps less emotionally compelling but fully authentic and God-honoring all the same. All this may take time, for it has to be *lived* through as well as *thought* through. What is required is a faithful patience, a willingness to see things through. Certainly this patience was exemplified in the life of Mother Teresa, whose faithfulness was extraordinary. We will, no doubt, need but a fraction of her patience — but we will need patience all the same. Unfortunately, it is the American way to want and expect a quick fix for any and all of our problems. We are not a patient people. If we don't get that quick fix, we are too often tempted to abandon our projects along with our hopes. Amidst our spiritual struggles, the best strategy may be simply to wait it out. As we do so, we pray for patience, as much as for light and an infusion of conviction, recognizing that these challenging times may not be over quickly. In praying for patience, we acknowledge, as with all trials of our faith, that we continue in God's providential hands and that we are embraced in his good purposes for our lives. There is nothing conceptually or psychologically odd in praying for patience to the very One who is the object of our uncertainty. For uncertainty does not mean there is no residue of belief, nor does it mean we can't pray in hope — for we can and by God's grace we will. Moreover, it is not that there is always something we must do (though I have made my suggestions) or some new grand insight that we must embrace (though I have offered these as well) so much as we should simply be, rest where we are, continuing faithful in our Christian walk and practice. At first this may be hard, but it gets easier as we move along and as time passes.

In the book of Genesis there is an intriguing and curious story of Jacob engaging in an extended wrestling match (Gen. 32:24-32). It's an all-nighter, ending only at the "break of day." Quite a strenuous undertaking when compared with those Olympic Greco-Roman wrestlers who are exhausted after three periods of two minutes each. What precipitated the match we are not told. The biblical narrative simply begins with the match in progress. It takes place in complete isolation. There is no referee awarding points and no cheering crowd of onlookers. The adversaries are completely alone, wrestling in the silence and darkness. Jacob's opponent, at first unidentified, turns out (apparently) to be God himself — certainly a formidable opponent. With God as Jacob's adversary, there appears to be no chance of victory. But when it comes to wrestling, Jacob is no slouch. He more than holds his own. When Jacob's opponent does not prevail, he takes recourse by putting Jacob's thigh out of joint, doing so by a mere touch. He thereby seeks an advantage over Jacob so that he can elude his grasp and depart before the break of day. But Jacob is not to be denied. He holds on to his adversary with all his might, preventing an escape. Jacob then declares, "I will not let you go unless you bless me." He receives the blessing and later exults, "I have seen God face-to-face, and yet my life is preserved."

But are we really, we may wonder, to believe that God could not defeat Jacob or escape his grasp and do so at will? This is God, after all, Jacob's creator and the creator of all things. Moreover, God put Jacob's thigh out of joint with a mere touch. Could he not with another touch weaken those strong muscles that held him in their vicelike grip? If we suppose that he could but did not, then — as we work with this story — we might construe this as a test for Jacob. How badly does he want that blessing? How badly does he want to see the face of God? To be sure, God places Jacob at a disadvantage, but he does not completely incapacitate him, as he easily could have. In essence, God says, "What are you going to do now, Jacob? Can you hold on to me with that dislocated thigh of yours? I could have incapacitated you far more, you know, but I didn't and I won't. The blessing can still be yours if you want it badly enough. All you have to do is hold on to me." And, of course, Jacob does want it badly enough. So he holds on with all his might and ultimately prevails. Dawn breaks and Jacob has his blessing. Jacob has seen the face of God.

We might take this wrestling match as a metaphor of the doubting believer, those of us who, as it were, wrestle with God and do so with our own dislocated thighs. Yes, we doubt and have been troubled by our doubts, but we are far from spiritually incapacitated. The match is not over yet. Just as Jacob of old could hold on to God, dislocated thigh and all, so can we. Like Jacob, we can receive the blessing and see the face of God. The key is holding on through our dark night. For us this means faithfully and patiently continuing in our normal Christian walk. We are not to allow God to elude our grasp by abandoning the things of God and simply letting go of God. Do we want God badly enough? That is the question that confronts us. Perhaps it is the question with which God, our adversary, confronts us. If the answer from our heart's deepest yearnings is yes, we will surely maintain our hold, and we will prevail. Daybreak may not come soon enough for our liking and the night for some may be long, but we are to hold on, ever mindful of the great prize that is within our grasp.

There is, however, another side to all this. Whereas God is our adversary, God is also our ally, wanting us to hold on, wanting us to prevail, wanting us to receive the blessing. We have a Helper as we wrestle. We do not wrestle alone. It may at times seem to us like complete darkness and isolation. And it may only be as one looks back that one sees that this was not so. And when we do receive the blessing and see the face of God, God himself will be pleased. This is what God wants for us. Our adversary wants us to be victorious, and in ways, perhaps hidden and beyond our full comprehension, God is at work willing it to be so.